The
SEMINARIAN

by
Michael Gillotti

D1534256

for
Shirley & Camina
who keep me filled up with love

**There is nothing more satisfying and fulfilling
than to dedicate oneself
to a cause greater
than oneself**

To Contact Michael Gillotti
visit website: www.michaelgillotti.com
or email: magill@sonic.net

Cover and Book Design by GabrielFraire.com

Contents

FORWARD

As I lay in bed one morning before getting up and starting my day, my mind wandered back to my days in the seminary. By entering the seminary I had committed myself to becoming a Roman Catholic priest. But why, I wondered. Why had I done it? What was going on at that time in my life that compelled me to make such a momentous decision?

My wife suggested that I write down some of these thoughts and memories about this very important and formative period of my life. Perhaps it would shed some light on who I am now and how I got here. This is where the story began, a few notes scribbled down that eventually took the shape of this memoir as more memories flooded in. It takes place during the tumultuous times of the civil rights movement and the anti-Vietnam War movement of the sixties and early seventies, both of which impacted me deeply and served to awaken my conscience.

It also takes place at a time when many long held beliefs and attitudes were being challenged. Everything was being questioned, including the authority of the Catholic Church. Priests and nuns were leaving religious life and, in many cases the Church itself, in record numbers. This was the back drop in which I began my religious training. And so, it was a bit incredible that there was no doubt in my mind that in eight years I would be ordained a Roman Catholic priest. My mind was made up. I was fully committed.

I went into it with my eyes wide open, or so I thought at the time.

Chapter 1

THE CALLING

It all started in eighth grade when Father Wingart arrived at St. Anthony's parish on the south side of Des Moines. He was young and handsome and drove a Chevy Impala convertible, not the usual car for a priest. He took me to the park to play tennis and took a few of us to a nearby lake to water ski. Occasionally he pulled me out of class and told me I was a leader, and took me and some others to dance lessons so we could teach our classmates. In short, he was cool. It was the first time I'd known a priest to be so. Usually they were unattractive and stern and fit a certain, well, you know, priest mold.

Perhaps that's when the seed was planted. I had never even considered it before, but now it became at least a possibility somewhere in my subconscious. Me become a priest, I don't think so, but if you could play tennis and water ski — maybe, just maybe.

But then I moved on to 9th grade at Dowling High School and soon forgot all about it. I was more interested in surviving my first year of high school, getting good grades and preparing myself for college, and of course, getting laid. Though the later was strictly forbidden, it didn't stop us from thinking about it often and on occasion even attempting it.

Few of us, if any, succeeded, but you'd never know this if you listened to the locker room stories after P.E. class. I think this was all made worse by the fact that I was in an all-male school and the Catholic girls' high school, St. Josephs, was on the other side of town. We had so little contact with the opposite sex during this period that it turned even shy and meek boys into raging maniacs.

It didn't help that the nuns at St. Joseph's took it upon themselves to protect their charges by drilling them regularly about the sinfulness and dangers of sex. They just completely ruined it for us. At the same time it was common knowledge that the Jewish girls at Roosevelt High School were not bound by the same restrictions that the Catholic girls were. There was hope!

But even this hope was fleeting. The priests at Dowling made it very clear that dating non Catholic girls was forbidden. This in turn led to long discussions about whether Jews were considered non-Catholic or whether they fell into an entirely different, and therefore, exempt category.

The Church was so determined to clearly define every rule, that it left open the possibility of getting around it by using its own narrow definitions and a little imagination. Take for example the term "prolonged petting." We were all very interested in the word "prolonged," since this is what elevated the entire affair from venial to mortal sin. And for those of you who were not Catholic, this was a huge distinction. It was the difference between a few years in purgatory with time off for good behavior and eventual ascension to heaven or, on the other hand, being condemned for eternity to hell.

So we were understandably concerned about just how long was considered "prolonged." One of the priests dared to tell one of his confessors (at least this is what she said) that anything under one minute was still a venial sin. After that we all lined up at his confessional on Saturday afternoon and kept our watches wound and within easy reach.

I suppose this part of the story would be incomplete if I didn't at least mention masturbation, since this was the most convenient and common method of expressing ones sexuality during adolescence. Predictably the Church not only classified it as sinful but placed it in the Mortal Sin Category. This was serious business because, as I found out later, 99% of adolescent boys masturbate during adolescence (I've never been very sure about the girls). In other words it's a perfectly normal and natural part of one's development.

How many of us, including myself, were tormented by guilt and then by the fear that we might die before Saturday, the day of Confession, and be thrown into the fires of hell forever? It was made crystal clear that once in hell, there was no escape. You could not get out for good behavior or by the help of others lighting candles and praying for you. It was PERMANENT.

Unfortunately, while I was going through this period of my life, I didn't have the perspective I have today. Back then I bought the whole package presented by the Church: I was a sinner and unworthy. If I didn't follow all the rules of the church, I would be condemned to an eternity in hell. If I missed mass on Sunday, for example and, earlier, if I ate meat on Friday, or if I stole more than one hundred dollars I had committed a mortal sin and would go straight to hell.

Generally, anything that felt good was forbidden and sinful. Bodily desires were to be resisted and controlled and distrusted. There was the sacred and then there was the profane. Sex definitely fell into the profane category, unless you were married and procreating and even then it remained a bit tainted.

But what if sex is a holy experience and not a profane one? What if it brings you closer to God and not closer to the devil? And what if it is to be celebrated and enjoyed? What if it's the closest we come to heaven on earth in the losing of ourselves in the ecstasy? The ego has a momentary loss of control and we are fully in the moment, united in body and spirit. Isn't that why people often shout out "Oh my God" during sex?

We are physical, emotional and spiritual beings. All three need to be acknowledged and honored. To be a healthy human is to find a balance between them. Making sex the forbidden fruit only serves to give it more power over us than what was intended or is healthy. Of course sex drives people to do things that are harmful to themselves or others and if we treat others inconsiderately or unkindly, there is always a price to pay. Otherwise we should enjoy it fully and try to develop a healthy and responsible attitude toward it.

I'm sure if you had asked my high school classmates, they would have agreed that I was not a likely candidate for the priesthood. I was handsome, outgoing, and athletic. Girls were attracted to me and vice versa. I had had sexual experiences with girls (though I never went all the way). So, when I let it be known in my junior year that I was planning to enter the seminary upon graduation, there was general disbelief. I learned later that many of the girls were actually heartbroken. It wasn't until I drove off to Dubuque in the fall of 1966 to start my studies that many classmates finally realized I was serious about it.

In a strange kind of way this is one of the reasons I chose the priesthood, precisely because I wasn't expected to. I thought that doing so would shock others into looking at their lives and help turn them into more kind and loving individuals.

There were many other things that drove my decision and chief among them was guilt, especially guilt around my sexuality. I felt I had used girls for my own sexual gratification without regard for them and their feelings. If there is such a thing as sin, this, I believe, is at its core — to do something for your own selfish satisfaction regardless of whether it is harmful to another or not. I had sinned and I felt horrible and guilty about it and I was seeking atonement. What better way than to give up all selfish desires and dedicate myself to the service of others.

The decision was also driven by the emotional pain I experienced witnessing my father verbally abuse my mother. He was never physical with her, but his words were violent and demeaning. Watching or listening to these recurring outbursts traumatized me and my siblings and we all suffered in our own way from it. Often the arguments were about money, or the lack of it, and my mother was always at fault for not better managing my father's irregular income.

Then there was the issue of my father's unfaithfulness. Of all the insults my mother endured from him, this was the cruelest of all. It was so egregious that I didn't want to believe it could be true. I rationalized away all the signs — literally the lipstick on his collar, the flirting, the late nights out and the rare occasion when my mother would confront him after a night out with another woman. In these situations he was masterful in turning the confrontation around so that he was the victim and she was the perpetrator. It was all done with a lot of anger, blaming and shouting, which I later came to see was nothing more than a big smoke screen to deflect the attention off his betrayal.

With every blowup the priesthood began looking more attractive. I wouldn't have to worry about money. I wouldn't have to deal with the difficulties of a relationship and marriage. As a priest I would be taken care of and all the stress and complexities of life could be avoided.

As a priest I would also be bringing enormous joy to my mother, grandmother and aunts, most of whom were very devout Catholics. Though I denied it at the time, it gave me great pleasure to know that I would be pleasing them. To have a son, grandson or nephew become a priest was a great honor to a family and, by the way, pretty much guaranteed their entrance into heaven. The men, on the other hand were a little more ambivalent about the value of having a priest in the family. They may have had a more realistic idea about what the priesthood was all about, or perhaps they considered a celibate man a bit strange.

One thing that was definitely not part of the attraction for me was all the rituals and colorful vestments. I know some of the other seminarians were really into all that and that some, as children, even dressed up like priests and said fake masses in their basements. Kind of like playing doctor, but with chalices instead of stethoscopes. But that was not me. Though I have to say, to this day I do love the smell of the incense wafting through the church on high holidays.

The priesthood was considered a vocation, and the parish priests, along with the teachers at Dowling were on the lookout for any young men that expressed an interest. You were "called" to the priesthood, they would say. In some ways it's not really your decision. God is calling. Your role is simply to respond. Even after all the driving forces mentioned above, there truly was something stirring inside me. There was the beginning of a realization that there's more to life than just the physical, material plane, and that true happiness derives not from the material but from the spiritual.

When Jesus was asked what were the greatest or most important commandments, he answered: To love God and to love your neighbor as you love yourself. These are the two great commandments. Perhaps I could help direct people toward these teachings and toward the realization of their own spiritual nature. Perhaps I could be an instrument in God's hands for the good of others. Yes, there was this inner calling along with all the other stuff that led me to one of the most difficult and important decisions of my life.

Toward the end of my senior year, after I was clearly committed and enrolled, I remember going to the corner of our backyard where we kept a 50 gallon metal barrel for burning trash. I pulled out all the high school wallet size photos of the girls I'd either dated or wanted to date and threw them into the fire. Though it was a dramatic gesture, it nonetheless seemed important to break clearly and completely with the past and move onto the future life in which I was embarking, which, of course, required that I give up physical sexual relations with the opposite sex.

There was no choice really. Celibacy was mandatory. It was part of the package, and I willingly and consciously chose to give up the pleasure of sex, marriage and family in order to dedicate myself to a higher purpose. Yes, I was giving up the girls, but I was willing to do this in order to accomplish a higher good. It was a serious and sober moment and one that I remember as if it were yesterday. I knew there was no doing this half way. I was all in!

Chapter II

ST. PIUS X SEMINARY LORAS COLLEGE

The Seminarian

My parents drove me up to Dubuque in the fall of 1966. They helped me unload my trunk and belongings at Rohlman Hall. I was in the first class in a while that was to attend Loras College and would not be sent to the remote Conception Seminary in Missouri. I didn't know at the time how lucky I was. At Conception seminarians had to wear cassocks and white Roman Collars and follow a more regimented schedule. Here we were on a liberal arts college campus and except for prayers in the morning and evening, could for the most part participate in campus activities. Walking several blocks down from the hilltop campus put you in downtown Dubuque.

As I said good bye to my parents, my mother started to cry. I knew that she was sad that I was leaving home and that this was a little more than just seeing your young son go off to college. She knew she was losing me to the religious life, to the life of a priest. I was God's child now.

Not wanting to have my own tears triggered, and not wanting to look too much like a "mamma's boy," I quickly went inside to get my room assignment. I knew on a certain level I now had to leave my family behind and get started on this new journey.

My roommate was already in our room when I arrived and had already unpacked.

"Hi, I'm Mike. What's your name?" I said with an extended hand.

"I'm Tom," he said, looking away as he took my hand.

I could tell immediately he was a shy farm boy. "Where you from, Tom?"

"Earlville."

"All right. Did you grow up on a farm?" I asked, though I already knew the answer.

"Yeah. We grew corn and soybeans. How about you, Mike?"

"I'm from Des Moines," I answered, trying to make it sound like the two places were equivalents.

Tom was the kind of kid that used to drive into Des Moines on weekends to mingle with the big city folks. We'd made fun of them and called them "hicks" or "farm boys." You could always spot them a mile away. Often they would "scoop the loop" around the downtown, looking a little lost or out of place. The "farmers' tans" and white socks also gave them away. We always looked down on them with a sense of superiority. We were the city kids. We knew what was happening. They didn't have a clue.

"So this is my roommate," I thought. I knew right from the start we would never be best friends, and I believe he did too. At the same time we both recognized that we were bound together in the same pursuit, we were both committing to a religious life of service.

Our room was small and sparely furnished. We each had our own bed, dresser and desk and shared space in the closet for our shirts and pants. My mother had marked all my clothing, including my underwear and t-shirts with a laundry stamp: M.GILLOTTI. So I unloaded these and other miscellaneous items, dragged my trunk up to the attic storage area and settled in to my new home.

THE STUDENT

Though I had been awarded the Aquinas Key, the highest academic award, upon graduating from Dowling High, I never considered myself very intelligent. I didn't fit in with all the other "brains" that were standing with me at the front of the chapel as we received our individual Aquinas Key pins. In some way I felt like a fraud. I just studied very hard, and as a result, got good grades, but I certainly wasn't smart.

I carried this same attitude with me to college and I remember feeling very inadequate and overwhelmed with the requirements of all the courses. The first year was very difficult for me and I studied long hours in my room and in the library just to keep up. At one point I was sure I was going to flunk out and I developed a pain in my left abdomen and frequent constipation. I started thinking about a backup plan in case I didn't make it here. I would join the Marines. They would make a man out of me!

I confided in the vice rector, Father Ede, my fears and abdominal pain. He referred me to an MD in town who, after examining me, declared there was no medical cause to my pain and prescribed some Valium. Ironically, the pain subsided before I even took one pill. This was my first direct experience with the power of the mind over the body, or what is commonly referred to as psychosomatics.

Father Ede then directed me to the psychologist on campus, another priest, Father Barta. While he was interviewing me, I broke down and started crying. "I'm worried about my father," I told him, "He's not well mentally. He's very neurotic and is in denial of reality."

"I can see that you're very worried about your father." he said.

"Yes, and I'm also frightened that he's behaving the way he does."

"What frightens you?" he asked.

"One thing is he 'goes off' on me or others over the smallest things. I've witnessed him vilify and demean people over nothing."

I later came to realize that though he wasn't an alcoholic, he was a rage-a-holic. As with an alcoholic, you were always a little apprehensive around him, not knowing when or what might trigger an episode of rage.

I know when it was directed toward me for some minor rule infraction, like not doing exactly what he told me to do, he would come down on me in such a way and with such intensity that I felt like a terrible person down to my core. In other words, it wasn't the behavior he was criticizing or objecting to, but the very essence of who I was. I felt completely invalidated as a human being. I also witnessed him doing this to many others, most frequently to my mother.

The other thing that concerned me was that he would often

deny he said what he just said or had just done. For example, if he was confronted about his rage toward someone, he would say, "I didn't do that, or I didn't say that, or I wasn't mad at that person," when just a moment ago he in fact did say that or do that. It just seemed really crazy to me, and it frightened and worried me terribly. Perhaps I worried that at some point he would go completely crazy like his younger brother, Ernie, who had been institutionalized off and on his entire life.

Father Barta listened to all of this but had the wisdom to see something else through all my tears and worry. "How do you feel about yourself?" He queried. I wasn't sure how to respond, so I answered, "I think ok." He wasn't buying it. "No," he continued, I heard all your concerns about your father, but what about you, what about your sense of self-worth, your own self esteem?"

I hadn't expected the session to go in this direction, but I trusted him enough to consider that he might be on to something. Though I had never put it those terms, I knew that there was something inside me that suffered, that wasn't quite right. Perhaps it was my sense of self-worth. Perhaps this is where I should be putting my attention and not on my father, as real and sad as his situation was.

We had several more sessions and they started me on a path of working on my own self-esteem, at recovering my own sense of self-worth. Ironically, it was lost in large part, but not entirely because of the Catholic Church itself. "Lord I am not worthy . . . Lord I am not worthy," had been droned into my head from early childhood. The fact that I was somehow a sinner from birth and continued to be one didn't help much either.

My self-esteem was also negatively affected by the family and larger social environment in which I grew up. There was a reluctance to praise a child or even to express one's love and affection for a child too much lest the child get "too big a head." Parents and others were always on the lookout for kids who felt too good about themselves and were quick to squash these notions before they got out of hand.

They didn't realize back then that there is a difference between an egotist who feels that he or she is "better" than anyone else, or is overly self-absorbed and someone who simply has a healthy sense of self-worth, one who simply feels good about who they are. I know for myself I didn't want a lot of over the top or undeserved praise, but a little acknowledgement once in a while would have gone a long way. People were a little stingy with their love and affection back then, and I know a lot of us suffered because of it.

Slowly I started to calm down and gain more confidence. "Maybe I can do this after all," I thought. I began to enjoy using my mind and learning, and before long was making the Dean's List.

I became a very serious student. Practically all I did was study. Initially it was out of fear of failure, then it evolved into the joy of learning. I'd start my day by walking across the abandoned football field, the Rock Yard, to the smaller of the two school cafeterias. It was reserved for seminary students. Then I was off to class. In between classes and after dinner, I would climb down to the basement level of the library where there were several small cubicles along the windowless walls. It was there that I established my home for the next four years.

Sitting for hours in my cubicle I learned how to study. I pushed and stretched my mind to places I didn't think I was capable of. I discovered new ideas, new areas of knowledge. It was hard work for me. Learning still didn't come easy or quickly, but it was coming.

I was fulfilling the basic goal of a liberal arts education. I was broadening my knowledge and understanding of the world around me and, at the same time, I was preparing myself for the priesthood.

Our seminary program was divided into two sections: Philosophy (undergraduate) and Theology (graduate), followed by an internship (practicing as a deacon in a parish) and ultimately Ordination into the Catholic Priesthood. So, at Loras the focus was Philosophy. Of course we took all the standard liberal arts classes as well, such as English, Biology, History, Speech, foreign language (ours was Latin) along with Philosophy.*

On the whole, these first four years of our training were much more about studying than about praying. Sure, we had evening prayers every night in the chapel at 10:00 PM, and there was mass on Sunday with talks from the Rector or Vice Rector on preparations for the religious life. There were even a few retreats thrown in at a nearby monastery, Mount Mellory. But by the end of our sophomore year most of these "spiritual" activities were no longer mandatory. I definitely felt more like a college student than a seminarian, and since we took all our classes alongside the rest of the

---

* See Seminary Schedule and Program, Seminary of St. Pius X, Loras College" in the Appendix, page 162, # 1.

college "lay" students, we were essentially indistinguishable from them.

We studied Plato, Socrates, Aristotle, Descartes, Existentialism, etc. It was all very heady and often abstract and conceptual. Though there was wisdom to be extracted from the great thinkers, I realized at one point that intellectually agonizing about the meaning of life can only get you so far. Reasoning your way to happiness wasn't very effective. In fact from what I could tell most of the philosophers were pretty miserable, victims of their own reasonableness and logic.

In an attempt to understand our essential nature, Descartes stated, Cognito ergo sum ("I think, therefore I am"). I'm sure he thought a lot about this beforehand. However, this requires that in order to exist one must be capable of thinking. Logically, if you don't or can't think, therefore you are not. But are we not also our feelings and, on a deeper level, are we not essentially spiritual beings?

Fortunately, I was rescued from all this "over-think" by a gentle Asian woman, Donan Wakefield. She taught a class called World Religions. She introduced me to the Eastern way of looking at life and religion. Before this I really had no interest in other religions. After all, we already had the one and only "true religion," Catholicism. We had the Pope and the direct lineage to St. Peter. We were the one true religion, we were told. All others were false religions or at the very least, lesser religions. This was made unequivocally clear during twelve years of Catholic Grade and High School.

So studying Hinduism, Buddhism, Taoism, Islam etc.

was a real eye opener. It was all so foreign and difficult to comprehend from my Catholic, Western mind. At the same time it was very interesting to me, and, in retrospect, opened my mind to this new world of Eastern thought and religion and started me on a journey of spiritual development based on an Eastern religious perspective. This ultimately led to the cultivation of a personal relationship with the higher power or God within each of us and away from the belief of and toward a direct experience of the divine. Who could have predicted I'd be doing Yoga and meditating within a year of graduating?

DANCING WITH THE DEVIL

It was 1966 when I arrived at Loras and as Dylan said, the times they were a changing.

There were thirteen seminarians from Dowling High, a new record. Randy Hill, Paul Douromis and a few others were pretty cool and experienced guys compared to many of our classmates, particularly those who had come from Minor Seminaries (high school seminaries). I felt sorry for them and they kind of looked to us as role models.

The cool guys' first brush with the old guard at the seminary came shortly after the school year began. Loras was at that time an all-male college (Here we go again with the separation of the sexes). They would have dances on campus with the all woman's college across town, Clark College. The three of us loved to dance and so we decided to go. When the Rector found out, the shit hit the fan. There were meetings and deliberations and all kinds of consternation. We were like, what's all the fuss about? We were just dancing. Apparently it was an unwritten rule and no one had ever violated it before, or perhaps not so openly.

As a credit to the Seminary leaders, they decided it was time to relax the rule a bit and allow us to go to dances. They didn't know it at the time, but this was the beginning of the end to practically all the rules that were in place. By the time we hit junior year, they had done away with mandatory prayers, the 10 PM curfew and even allowed women to visit our dorm rooms.

Of course, underneath their concerns about dancing was the issue of celibacy. There were no formal vows taken at this time, but it was assumed that if you were in the seminary you would be celibate. The formal vows would come later.

As I mentioned earlier, I was perfectly willing to be celibate and took the commitment very seriously. So I listened with great interest as we were coached on how to pull this off (no pun intended). One suggestion that stands out is the exercise of "sublimation."

I'd never heard the term before and at first it sounded a little like masturbation, so I was dismayed to find out it was just the opposite. It was taking all that sexual energy that wells up inside us that makes us want to have sex and doing something else with it that was not sexual. It all sounded pretty reasonable until they gave an example. When the urge starts to well up inside, find a friend and go play handball.

I laugh when I think of it now and am not sure if I should laugh or cry when I realize after all these years, after all the priests that fled the priesthood, after all the child molestation, after the declining enrollment in seminaries, the Church is still not willing to drop the requirement of celibacy for their priests. In my mind it's totally unnecessary to fulfilling the duties of a priest and, in fact, may be a detriment. Even more absurd is the fact that the Catholic leadership has forbidden even the discussion of the subject.

Traditionalists argue that celibacy is a traditional institution that can't and shouldn't be changed. Surely they are aware that in the early days of the church, and my understanding is until around 1100 AD, priests in fact were allowed to be married. There were even instances where popes were married and/or had children.

On the other side there's the psychological argument for doing away with it. I believe it goes something like this: The expression of one's sexuality and physicality is a normal and necessary activity for one's mental health. To repress or suppress or sublimate these desires is unhealthy. It's a strain on the psyche and, in some cases can lead to deviant type behaviors such as molestation and pedophilia. In other words, if you don't express it directly, it will come out in strange and unhealthy ways that can be harmful to oneself and others.

All these realizations came to me much later. At the time I willingly accepted the requirement. I know it might sound crazy, but in retrospect it was actually a good thing for me.

Perhaps because I had made such a firm commitment, it really wasn't that difficult. Even masturbation was rare, and when it did happen, was somewhat embarrassingly confessed to my personal confessor, the Vice Rector. I had it all under control.

Once when I was visiting some friends in Des Moines, one asked me about this. "Don't you get horny?" he quizzed.

I answered honestly, "Not really. I'm giving it up for a higher cause."

He didn't believe me. Then I added, "Besides, they secretly add salt peter to our meals. It takes the edge off."

Though I could offer no evidence of this occurring, I'm pretty sure they believed me. How else could someone do without it?
"Still, don't you just want to screw someone sometimes?" he added.

The others jumped all over him for even broaching the subject. They felt he was being disrespectful to a future priest. I took it all in stride.

Although I now criticize the Church for continuing to mandate their priests be celibate, it did serve me in an important way. I learned self-discipline. I learned that I have the ability to exert my will over all the random desires and impulses that pass my way. This becomes important in everyday life where we are bombarded with seductive invitations daily around food, sex, alcohol, drugs, cigarettes, money, etc. We are constantly being told to indulge ourselves. Without some self-discipline it's very easy to slip into overindulgence and even addiction, which in turn can lead to other serious mental and physical problems. Of course, none of this applies to an occasional well-made chocolate covered donut.

ROCKY MOUNTAIN HIGH

There were a few seminarians from Colorado in our class and after our freshman year they invited a handful of us to come to their home state for the summer to help out at a youth camp up in the mountains in southern Colorado. Having never seen a mountain before it sounded very exciting and adventurous to me.

Randy, Paul and I signed up. The only catch was we had to get ourselves there. After that they would feed and house us and give us $50 a month, not a lot of money, even back then. Randy's mother just happened to catch a bulletin board announcement on Bill Riley's TV show about a man, Claus Johnson, who was moving his family to New Mexico and needed someone to drive a moving van and another car out there along with his wife and daughter. He would meet us in New Mexico and fly us to Colorado in his private plane.

Now it was beginning to sound even more exciting, especially since he was moving to a ranch that his son was managing near Roswell and we could spend a couple days there rounding up cattle and such before he flew us north.

Since I was used to driving my dad's four-speed ¾ ton pickup, I was assigned to drive the moving van. I soon learned it was a little trickier than a pick up. It had a two-speed axel, which was engaged with a little red knob on the gearshift. The owner showed me how to shift it, but I kept grinding the gears anyway and was very embarrassed. Randy had it easy he drove a Ford sedan with automatic transmission.

The plan was to caravan to New Mexico, with the wife and daughter traveling in the lead car. I would follow in the van and Randy would bring up the rear. Everything started out smoothly enough and I quickly figured out the transmission. But apparently the wife hadn't been trained on caravanning and all the rules that apply to this operation, the most important of which is to keep the other vehicles behind you in view and in close proximity. By the time we hit Kansas City she was so far ahead of me that I couldn't see her.

The next thing I remember was a very confusing intersection with road construction in progress. I turned left and ended up on a two lane highway heading to who knows where.

She, I later found out turned right onto the Kansas Turnpike. Randy followed me. After a few miles I realized my error and turned around.

Randy pulled his Ford up behind me. We were both distraught. "What the hell happened?" Randy said somewhat accusingly.

"I couldn't see her. The signs were all so confusing. She must have gone the other direction," I pleaded, really wanting it to be her fault and not mine.

"What are we gonna do?" Randy said frantically. "We don't even know where we're going."

At that moment it hit us hard. Neither one of us had gotten the name or address of her husband's son. We were in a hell of a predicament. And I was the one who had made the wrong turn. I felt responsible for the whole thing.

"She must have gotten on the Kansas Turnpike," I said rapidly, my mind racing. "I'll never catch up with her in this slow truck. You've got to get back to the turnpike and floor it. I'll try to find you somehow," I ordered.

"It's hopeless," Randy said. "We'll never catch her."

"We've got to. Go 90 or 100 or whatever it takes. You've got to catch her or we're screwed," I shouted.

Randy and I rushed off and when we hit the turnpike he sped off ahead of me.

I cranked the big truck through the gears as fast as I could, but he was soon out of sight.

It was a hot summer day but my sweat was not heat induced. It was severe guilt and embarrassment induced. I beat myself up over and over again. "How could I be so stupid? Look what a mess I've caused! But she should have stayed closer to me. I'm not the only one to blame here," I argued with myself.

While this circular argument ran round and round in my head I nearly drove right past Randy's big red Ford. I pulled over up ahead of him and jumped out of the truck, and as I approached him, shouted, "What are you doing? Why did you stop?" I said angrily.

"I can't do this," he said.

"We've got to catch her," I insisted. "You're giving up too soon."

"Look, what do you want me to do? I could get a ticket or get in an accident. The whole car was shaking."

After I calmed down a little I knew he was right. It was futile. We got back into our vehicles and drove a few miles to the next rest stop, unsure how this was all going to turn out. To make things worse we were counting on our travel expenses being paid by the wife so had very little money on us. I don't think we had more than $20 between us.

We saw a highway patrolman pull into the rest area and, desperate, we approached him and told him our predicament. He radioed ahead to the next rest stop and much to our relief, the wife was waiting for us there. I was still feeling very bad when we met up with her but she didn't seem to be too upset, so we started off again toward the west, happy that this unpleasant event was behind us.

But unfortunately, the wife hadn't learned the lesson. She violated the cardinal rule of caravanning again and was soon out of sight. Only now it was getting dark and I was getting mad again. To compound matters the headlights and taillights of the truck were blinking on and off and then went off altogether. Around that time I saw the wife several cars ahead but couldn't catch her, even though I held the gas pedal all the way to floor. So out of fear for my own safety I pulled off at a hotel, hoping she would see me. She didn't. Randy followed me and was angry as hell at me for pulling over. I was angry at the wife for violating the caravan rule. We were both complete wrecks. How could this be happening again? We decided to get a room and hope for the best tomorrow.

We got up the next morning and called the highway patrol. Sure enough she had done so also and was waiting in the next town. When we met up this time I wanted to give her a piece of my mind but instead suppressed it. This was before I took all the workshops on the importance of expressing one's anger, and besides, we were totally vulnerable and dependent on her. We did manage to get a name and address of the son in New Mexico this time and we rolled out again. Only now we were limited to daytime driving. The truck's lights were completely unworkable. This slowed us down considerably and delayed our arrival date by a day or so.

Having seen lots of cowboy movies as kids, Randy and I both had a pretty good idea what to expect at the ranch. First of all there would be a long ranch house with a horse barn and a corral of horses nearby. I was picturing something like the Ponderosa Ranch on Bonanza. We were also told there was a swimming pool and after all this traveling, we were really looking forward to a cool dip.

After driving through a long and dusty ranch road and through a few dried up riverbeds, we finally pulled up to the ranch house. Randy and I were dumbstruck. It was nothing like we pictured. The house was old, small and unpainted. The pool was nothing more than a rusting watering tank for the horses and was only about three feet deep. They showed us to the bunkhouse. It was dark and dirty and the beds were thin and uncomfortable. What a disappointment.

Claus came up to us the next day and told us that since we would be here for a couple days, we would have to paint the bunkhouse. Randy was irate. "We didn't sign up for this," he complained. "The guy's taking advantage of us."

I was ok with the painting and tried to calm him down, "He did get us this far without costing us anything." I argued. "What's the big deal doing a little painting?"

"This is a bunch of shit," he grumbled, and reluctantly grabbed a paint brush.

I was always so nice and accommodating. It has its advantages, but sometimes I wish I had a little more of Randy's spirit. To this day I admire Randy for the way he stands up for himself and doesn't take any shit from anyone. It's never come easy for me but I'm learning.

He mellowed out later when the son took us on a horseback ride to check on the cattle. This was more like it. Now we could live out our cowboy fantasies. The problem was the ranch was so huge, we never did see any cattle. We rode around for a while then came back and took a dip in the pool/watering tank.

That night the son and his friend took us out for some

nighttime hunting. They had a high-powered rifle and a powerful spot light on the top of their pick up. Randy and I and the friend rode in the back while the son shone the spot light on our first victim, a jackrabbit, which was blinded and frozen by the bright light. The friend blew it apart. Next was a porcupine, which was also obliterated by the high-powered rifle. It was all great fun and entertainment to them, so when they offered us the rifle, we accepted.

I'm a little fuzzy about what happened next, but I think I shot something. I say something, because after the shooting, there was so little left of the animal it was hard to identify. Though I had hunted pheasants, squirrels and rabbits as I was growing up, this was an entirely different ballgame. There was something unsettling about this kind of "hunting," this killing for sport. At the same time I didn't want to appear unmanly to the two cowboys, so I didn't say a word.

The next day we loaded up Claus's twin-engine plane and squeezed into the narrow back seat. We had offered to take Paul's trunk with us and Claus wasn't pleased. He was concerned that the extra weight would make it difficult to take off and to avoid the trees at the end of the short gravel runway, if you could call it a runway. Randy and I both held our breath as he revved the engines while holding the plane back with the brake. The plane shook violently. Finally, when the engines were roaring at a high RPM, he released the brake and we were catapulted down the runway. We cleared the trees, but barely. He circled the ranch once, waved to his son and we were off.

The excitement of riding in a private plane soon evaporated as we began passing over the Rockies near the

Colorado border. The turbulence was unrelenting and I was on the verge of vomiting. Claus handed me a coffee can with a lid and shortly afterward I emptied my stomach. It didn't help my motion sickness at all. I was pale and sick the entire flight. I was expecting a little sympathy from Claus when we landed. I was too sick to deal with the coffee can so left it in the plane. Claus grabbed it and shoved it toward me.

"Don't expect me to deal with this. Take it into the bathroom and clean it out!" He ordered.

I took the smelly can unenthusiastically and mumbled under my breath as I walked away, "What an ass. Can't he see I'm sick?"

Father John, the organizer of the summer camp, met us at the airport and drove us to Alamosa. I realized at that point that there was probably an ulterior motive to inviting us to help with the summer camp. Turns out he was the vocational director of the Pueblo Diocese. Perhaps if we liked Colorado enough we would consider dumping the Des Moines Diocese and transferring to Colorado. This was a little deceptive, I thought, but I didn't care. I was in the Rocky Mountains. What a high!

We met our fellow counselors, most of whom were Colorado seminarians, and spent that first night on mattresses spread out on the basement floor of the Alamosa church rectory. In the morning we piled into the church's 1957 Ford station wagon and were driven up to the campsite. The camp, we learned was a two hour drive up into the Sangre De Christo Mountains. The road was windy and treacherous, with shear drop offs and no guard rails. We were all a little pale when we arrived at the campsite.

The camp was nestled into a small meadow with steep mountain walls all around and the mountain fed Alamosa River running along one side. It was stunning. What a thrill it was to be in the mountains.

The cabins were small and "rustic" with three bunk beds somehow squeezed into each one. The counselors slept on an army cot near the entrance. The head counselor stayed in a small A-Frame cabin with a fireplace. There was no electricity or plumbing. This was before Porta-Potties and the site made outhouse was beyond gross.

Besides the awesome beauty of the camp, here's what I remember the most about the summer: freezing and starving to death. First the freezing. We were in the mountains and it got real cold at night. I slept with all my clothes on in a very old and thin wool sleeping bag. I may as well have been naked, for the cold penetrated down to the bone.

I would get out of bed each morning and stand outside with the others shivering and watching the sun move ever so slowly down the western slope until it bathed us in its warm rays. It took another hour or so to thaw out, but before this process was complete, we would huddle around the cook's cabin to receive our breakfast. This is where the starving part comes in.

Most mornings it was a very small box of breakfast cereal and milk. Cereal companies used to make these small, aluminum foil lined boxes that also served as bowls.

You just opened up the face of the box, poured in some milk and ate away. Because the previous eight hours of shivering burned so many calories, one box was woefully inadequate to support human life. But one box was all there was. The Parish was on a tight budget.

We all quickly became sleep deprived and chronically hungry and as a result very irritable. So when Randy quietly slipped into the heated A frame for a week to sleep, this didn't go over very well with me or the other staff members.

"How come you get to sleep in comfort while the rest of us are freezing?" I asked him accusingly.

"I didn't have any kids in my cabin this week. What's the big deal?"

"Well you could have offered to trade off a night or two. It's colder than shit out here." I responded.

"Lay off of him," Paul interjected. "You know we have to stay in the cabins with our kids. He didn't do anything wrong."

I stewed about this injustice for a few days but then let it go. It was just too beautiful up there in the mountains and I was grateful to be there. However, the cook must have heard about this encounter and knew how to soothe our wounds. That week on her wood burning stove she made pancakes for everyone.

Though the camp was very primitive and ill equipped, it did provide a wonderful experience for the kids. Most were 7th and 8th graders from poor, Hispanic families.They would have never been able to send their kids to summer camp. The diocese generously picked up the tab.

New kids were brought up in the station wagon every Monday and driven back on Saturday. A new batch was then brought up. The counselors returned to the parish on Saturday with the kids so were able to recuperate in the luxurious basement of the rectory and take a shower before returning on Monday and starting all over again.

On one return trip a counselor brought back a couple of watermelons. Since the Alamosa River was fed by melting snow from nearby mountains, the water was ice cold.

Someone decided that it would be a good idea to put the watermelons in the river to cool them off before we ate them. They were placed near some rocks and seemed to be staying put as the river rushed swiftly by. As we walked away we heard some loud shrieks near the riverbank.

The melons had broken free from their "port" and were very quickly being washed down stream.

"Quick kids. Get the melons before they get away!" John, the lead counselor shouted.

"There they are, there they are," one of the kids yelled. "Grab them! Grab them!"

"Don't let them go," another camper cried out, as the melons bobbed and rolled swiftly down the stream.

Soon we were all running at full speed along the river

bank, fighting our way through the thick brush while keeping our eyes on the watermelons. The kids were having a great time. The counselors were all thinking, "we're losing our precious dessert."

Just when it looked like the river was winning the race, we heard a big splash.

"I've got one," we heard one of the counselors yell as he dragged himself up the river bank.

We were all relieved that he had retrieved one of the melons and were grateful for his cold numbing plunge. But what about the second melon.

"I'm afraid it's lost forever to the rapids," he said. "Hopefully someone downstream will enjoy it."

And boy did we enjoy the one he saved. It was the best tasting water melon I've ever eaten! The watermelon chase also provided us with lots of smiles and laughs for days afterward.

Almost every night we lit a campfire and Paul would pull out his guitar and lead us in campfire songs, like *Kumbaya* or *Where Have All the Flowers Gone.* This was really the best part of the day and I enjoyed singing with the kids and counselors. I also began to notice how much fun Paul was having playing guitar and leading the singing. I'd never played a musical instrument before and knew nothing about music, but that summer I vowed I'd learn to play the guitar.

At the end of the summer we had a few days to play

before heading back home. The head counselor, John, invited Randy and me to accompany him in climbing a nearby mountain, Caneos Peak. If I remember correctly, it was around 13,000 feet and we were both very jazzed to have the opportunity for yet another adventure.

The first night we built a lean-to from branches and spread leaves on the ground for our beds. We reached the tree line (11,000 feet) the next day around noon. There was a little rock climbing but mostly it was just walking up a very, very steep mountainside. I learned a new term, "switch- backing." Climbing straight up was nearly impossible and used too much energy, so we walked back and forth horizontally and gradually moved up the mountainside.

Walking through snow the last few hundred feet, we summited late afternoon. All you could see for miles were more mountain peaks. We drank from narrow streams flowing off the snowmelt. We were higher than a kite!

The air was thin and we all had trouble breathing. Our guide, John, was a little nervous about getting caught on the mountain after dark, so he led us quickly down, back tracking our steps. Randy's legs and mine were killing us even more going down than up and we kept pleading with John, "Our legs are hurting. Can't we stop and rest a bit?"

"No," he answered. "We can't risk it getting dark up here. We've got to hurry down!"

He then continued to plunge down the mountainside, leaving us behind, aching and frustrated. I said to Randy, "This is really pissing me off. It looks like there's a lot of light left."

"That's what I say. But we've got to stay with him or we're liable to get lost."

Thankfully, we all got down safely just as the sun was setting. What a memorable experience. Not only had we been able to be "in" the mountains the past couple months, we were also able to actually climb one. And what a great way to end our summer in Colorado!

Soon after our climb we got a ride to Denver where we spent the night. We were then given $20 a piece for bus fare back to Iowa. Randy and I decided to pocket the money and hitchhike back home. Twenty dollars could go a long way back then and we needed it. Why waste it on the bus?

Fortunately, we got a ride all the way to Des Moines so didn't have to camp along the road. A few days later we were back in Dubuque, where we carried our "Rocky Mountain High" into our sophomore year.

Apparently while we were in Colorado, one of our more enterprising classmates, John Lugwig, must have gone to Barber School. He was now offering hair cuts in the basement for 50 cents a cut. Unfortunately, in our senior year his business fell off dramatically. By then we weren't really getting hair cuts much. Long hair was in. Short hair was out, like everything else.

Chapter III

THE RADICAL

It was nearly impossible not to be affected by the two great struggles of the 1960's: Civil Rights and the Vietnam War. They were in the air and on the airwaves. Young people as well as adults were putting their bodies and lives on the line. Songs were being written, demonstrations were happening on nearly every campus. My involvement with both issues directly derived from my study of Christ's life and teachings, which both informed and compelled my involvement.

THE CIVIL RIGHTS MOVEMENT

Gradually my conscience and my consciousness were awakened. I'd seen Martin Luther King Jr. leading marches, and seen the brutality the police rained down on the demonstrators, the water cannons and dogs and beatings. I heard Peter, Paul and Mary sing *Blowin In the Wind*. It all had an impact. I knew in my heart that no one should be treated that way, that we were all endowed with a common humanity regardless of the color of our skin, that no one was superior or inferior to anyone else.

Our shameful history of slavery and segregation had to be corrected if we were going to be true to our principles as expressed in the Declaration Of Independence, that all men "are created equal." If we are going to be true to our Christian faith that all are created in the image and likeness of God, then every person, regardless of the color of their skin, deserves to be treated accordingly.

Word got out on campus that Father Groppi was leading civil rights marches in Milwaukee to end housing and employment discrimination. A couple of buses were rented and many of us signed up to join Father Groppi over the weekend. I was happy to be taking some concrete action to end segregation and discrimination and not just talking about it.

Shortly before the weekend I called home and let my parents know that I would be joining the march. My father went ballistic.

He kept yelling, "How old are you? How old are you?"

It was a rhetorical question. I knew he knew but I answered anyway, "I'm twenty."

"Then you still have to obey me," he said, "you're not twenty one yet. I forbid you to go."

"Well, I have to go," I responded. "I have to do my part."

The next thing I know I'm called into the office of the Rector of the Seminary, Father Leonard. "Sit down." he said. "Your father just called me and was very upset that I was allowing you to go to Milwaukee for this civil rights march. He feels it would be too dangerous for you. He was so angry that I'm afraid if you defy him and go, I may have to suspend you from the seminary."

"But it feels important to go," I answered. "A lot of us are going. It's not really that dangerous."

"I understand your feelings and they are good and idealist, but I must insist you don't go!" he responded.

I felt humiliated and was furious that my father had intervened in this way. I was incredulous that he had called the Rector and embarrassed that he had chewed him out. This was my seminary and my Rector. He had no right to use the Rector to put me in my place. It created a huge rift between us that took years to heal.

I was torn and spent a lot of time reflecting on what I should do. Should I follow my conscience or obey my father and avoid being suspended. I hated that he had put me in this position. In the end it felt important to take a stand, both for civil rights and for myself. I decided I would go anyway and risk the consequences.

As fate would have it there was a gigantic snowstorm that weekend and the bus trip was cancelled. My seminary training along with my relationship with my father, though strained, was preserved, at least until the next storm.

In 1967 there were terrible riots in major U.S. cities fueled by the inequities between the races. Whole areas of Detroit, Chicago, LA and others were in flames and there was serious looting, injuries and deaths. The National Guard was called in to try to restore order. A commission was set up to study the causes and a paperback book released with the results. It was widely read on campus. The whole thing was very disturbing.

Not only was Loras an all-male college, it was for all practical purposes, an all-white college. However, we did have a handful of black students and they too were caught up in the times. They were demanding a Black Cultural Center be set up on campus and were poised for confrontation.

One day in the cafeteria I saw several white students wearing some kind of wooden icons around their necks. They explained that they had formed a group called White Students for Black Power. I joined the next week though never did get a totem. As tensions were rising we all met with several black students in one of the dorm rooms. The blacks were angry that one of them had been kicked off the basketball team because he had an Afro hairdo. They wanted to go into the chapel the next day and disrupt the mass and seemed intent on causing some destruction there and other areas on campus. I pleaded with them not to do this and that a non-violent demonstration would be more effective.

They reluctantly agreed and we came up with a plan. The next day around fifteen of us went to the mid-day mass and stood in the back of the chapel. When it came time for the offertory, we all walked to the front of the room. I immediately moved to the lectern and I read the following statement:

As our offertory prayer today we support the black

students in their demand for the reinstatement of the basketball player that was removed from the team and their demand that a cultural center be set up on campus . . .

The priest and the attendees (only a handful) were shocked. This only served to encourage us, so we then marched out and down to the faculty dining hall where we marched through chanting the demands of the black students. The priests and other faculty who were eating their lunch were not amused. Again, another shock wave.

I was pleased with how it turned out and especially that there was no violence or destruction. The next day in the Dubuque newspaper there was an article about how I'd "seized the microphone and yelled out the black students' demands" and how we had harassed and insulted the faculty. Myself and two of the black students were brought before the disciplinary board where we were interrogated and threatened with expulsion.

This time I was worried. I was naïve enough to think it wouldn't be this serious.

I was told later that the board was split. Some wanted us thrown out immediately and some wanted a lesser penalty. In the end they put us all on probation with a warning. They made it clear that one more incident and they would be compelled to expel us.

On my next trip back to Des Moines the bishop also called me in and lectured me about the inappropriateness and disrespectfulness of our actions. He said, "I read the newspaper article and was briefed by the seminary Rector about what happened last month and I'm very concerned. Though I appreciate your social conscience and desire to act for civil rights, I don't condone or encourage these kinds of protests. It's particularly disrespectful to bring this kind of thing into the holy mass!"

I had no real response and feared I might lose my position in the seminary, so said rather meekly, "Yes bishop. It won't happen again."

Though I may have been discouraged from future action at this time, the cause of civil rights and justice continued to be a cause close to my heart.

VIETNAM

**Draft Information Table next to
Army Recruitment Table, 1969**

Not only had I bought the whole package regarding the authority of the Catholic Church without questioning, I had also done the same with the U. S. Government. If the experts and authorities of the government determined that we needed to fight a war in Vietnam, then it must be done without questioning. They knew better than we.

When I entered the seminary I was fully willing to put on a uniform and fight for my country whenever and wherever they choose to send me. I knew nothing about Vietnam except that we had to be there to stop communism. That was good enough for me. And as I mentioned earlier, if this seminary thing didn't work out, my backup plan was to join the Marines. They would make a man out of me and I could make my mark in the glorious arena of war.

That all changed early in my sophomore year as I was walking through the seminary lobby. A group of students were gathered around one of the older seminarians, Chuck, arguing about pacifism and conscientious objectors. The older man had been in the Navy and was now arguing that the right position of a Christian was to abstain from participating in war.

"How can one say they are following the teachings of Jesus to love our neighbor as our self and then kill that neighbor?" He argued. "And what about the Old Testament commandment, thou shall not kill?" He added.

He then went into the whole Vietnam situation, proclaiming, "The Gulf of Tonkin incident in 1964 was merely a pretense to justify an authorization of war. We had no business interfering with the internal affairs of another sovereign nation."

The other students argued that we needed to stop communism and that pacifist were nothing but cowards. They threw all the standard clichés at him. "What would you do if your grandmother was being raped or attacked? Would you just stand there?" And, "If Vietnam goes communist, there would be a domino effect pushing other countries in the area into the communist fold."

This very emotional confrontation in the lobby had an immediate impact on my thinking. I had never considered any of this before. I had been taught for years that killing another human being was murder and a mortal sin punishable by an eternity in hell. But if you put on a uniform and kill another, you were somehow exempt from this moral dictate and in fact, would be considered a great patriot and even a hero.

Now I began to see that by being in the military you have surrendered your own will to the will of another authority, your commanding officer. I began to question what it does to your soul to be put in a situation where you're required to follow an order to kill and to ignore your own conscience and inner moral code. By injuring another, are we not also injuring ourselves? By killing another, are we not killing a part of ourselves, does not a part of us die also?

Though there was no name for it at the time, it is now known as "moral injury" (this is in addition to and different than the widespread Post Traumatic Stress Disorder, PTSD) and is a serious problem for returning vets who have a difficult time reconciling who they are at their core with what they did or witnessed being done.

And then there was the issue of Vietnam itself. How did we get involved there and what were we doing there, not to mention where the hell is it? I began to question it all.

A short time after witnessing this hallway argument, my roommate, Tom Lindsley and I had a conversation about the war. He was already far, ahead of me in his thinking. "I'm going to start the process of filing for conscientious objector status with my draft board," he informed me.

"But why?" I responded. "We have seminary deferments(4D)."

"I know. But I want to make a statement. I want to take a stand against war."

"But isn't it risky, Tom?" I responded. "What if they don't give you the new classification?"

"I'll still have my 4 D classification. They'll only take action to reclassify if there's a change in my status. As long as I'm in the seminary or an ordained priest, I'll keep my 4 D classification. Besides, it's the right thing to do if I want to call myself a Christian and a follower of Jesus Christ. To love and to kill were fundamentally contradictory."

Everyone at Loras College and colleges and universities all over the country were having similar conversations, less the seminary aspect. We were all trying to figure out how we would deal with the war and with the draft. Some decided to volunteer for the army hoping it would give them some leverage in where they were assigned. Others decided to go to Canada and escape the draft and the war altogether. The Canadian government offered little resistance to this scheme and as a result thousands crossed our northern border and into Canada.

Still others decided to go underground, fake illnesses, mental and physical or had their family doctor write them notes or, as in the case of George Bush, use their family connections to get them into the National Guard, where you were presumably unlikely to be sent to Vietnam. Those who couldn't make up their minds simply allowed themselves to be drafted, hoping for the best.

For those unfamiliar with the situation we confronted, our relationship to the draft and war was not an academic exercise. All young men 18 and older were required to register for the draft and draft boards throughout the country had the authority to draft anyone at any time. There were some exceptions, such as medical problems and, of course, student deferments, which allowed you to complete college. Otherwise the draft board owned you. Up until this era their authority over you was rarely if ever questioned.

President Johnson needed young bodies to implement his plan of "shock and awe." He was convinced that if the Vietnamese saw and felt the impact of the U.S. war machine, the small little peasants in pajamas would be so intimidated they would be eager to surrender. As history revealed, he totally underestimated their tenacity and nationalistic spirit.

He needed a minimum of 500,000 troops to accomplish this, and since the rotations at that time were thirteen months, he needed to constantly replenish the cannon fodder. We all knew we could only postpone but never escape the draft and, likely, Vietnam.

As stories and photos emerged of what we were actually doing to the people and countryside of Vietnam, opposition to the war grew. I remember when the reality of the brutality we were perpetrating on the Vietnamese hit me. This was not a noble and glorious war to save the world from communism. It was mass murder and destruction and the soldiers fighting there knew it.

I'll never forget the photos published worldwide of the My Lai Massacre. The bloody bodies of men, women and children seen lying in ditches along the road, the burning huts. What kind of monster would do this? In all, 500 civilians were massacred that day by U.S. soldiers.

Then there were the photos of old men and women and their children running naked and terrified down the road, napalm sticking to their skin burning anything and anyone randomly. There was one very compelling photo of a young naked girl, Kim Phuc, running down the road with much of her skin burned off from a napalm bomb. She is now a grown woman and has been on the news. She still suffers from her wounds all these years later and she is constantly undergoing laser treatments to reduce her scars and pain. What was her crime?

I wanted nothing to do with this madness and I grew angrier and angrier at our government and especially President Johnson and Defense Secretary Robert McNamara and later Richard Nixon for their callousness and for the effect the war was having on the Vietnamese as well as our own soldiers.

A couple of my classmates were killed and others came back traumatized and changed forever. One of my friends, Joe, shared some of the horrors with me after he returned. "The war turns guys into animals," he said. "I saw soldiers cutting off ears and other body parts and hanging them off their belts. They would just go nuts. They'd carve their platoon number into dead corpses."

I wanted to be sensitive to him and not ask too many questions that would bring up bad memories. Still I wanted to know from someone who had been there what was actually happening. "It sounds like hell. I'm sorry you had to go through that."

"It's worse than hell," he continued. "I saw guys raping women and some of the Vietnamese kids would come into the camps and sell their sisters to the soldiers for sex."

He was particularly distraught by the fact that he had killed women, children and old men as a sniper shooting into "free kill zones," where you were ordered to kill anything that moved. Then there was the time he threw a grenade into a tunnel after young kids had run into it for protection. I'm sure there were many more things that he was unwilling or unable to share with me. Working at a hospital after returning he would fall to the floor when he heard the sound of a canister shooting through the pneumatic tube system.

Like many other vets, he has PTSD and recurrent nightmares.

As the war dragged on and the whole concept of "victory" became ever more elusive, the morale of the soldiers plunged. They weren't there to bring democracy to Vietnam now. They were there to survive their tour and help their buddies to survive as best they could. Drugs and alcohol were prevalent.

It was hell on earth. You never knew who or where the enemy was. Days were filled with tension and sleep was hard to come by. If an officer got too eager to take them out on patrol, they made sure an "enemy" grenade ended up in his tent. It was called "fragging."

We dropped more bombs on Hanoi and North Vietnam, and later Laos and Cambodia, than were dropped in all of World War II. Napalm was used extensively and stuck to and burned everything around, including human skin. The American dead were broadcast on the nightly news, but the Vietnamese killed, like so many other aspects of the war were kept concealed. As a result we don't know for sure how many were killed. Most reports I've read say a minimum of 2 million and as high as 4 million were killed. This does not count the maimed and injured, nor the vast destruction of the countryside, nor the loss of limbs, birth defects or the diseases contracted for years after the war ended from land mines and all the chemical defoliants that were used.

We dropped over 12 million gallons of Agent Orange, for example and 20 million gallons of other herbicides. Agent Orange contained the chemical Dioxin and in some areas of South Vietnam today the Dioxin levels are 100 times international standards. The Vietnam government estimates that there are more than 4,000,000 victims of Dioxin poisoning alone!

At the end of their tour soldiers were expected to forget everything they did and witnessed and return to civilized society. We know now that this was impossible for many. Drugs, alcohol, depression, anxiety and violence returned with them. A high percentage of homeless street people are or were Vietnam Vets, and we now have passed a milestone no one should be proud of or celebrating. There have now been over 58,000 suicides of returning Vietnam Vets. More have killed themselves than died in Vietnam.

These suicides as well as the many other problems of

Vietnam Vets are the tragic result of training men to kill a dehumanized enemy, in this case the "VC" or the "Gooks." In the process they often lost part of their humanity as well. A friend shared with me that during his infantry training the dehumanization included chanting repeatedly: "Kill, Kill, I want to go to Vietnam, I want to kill some Vietcong." The military may try to make a distinction, but killing for one's country is in the end, still what it is, the taking of another human being's life. This is not easily erased from one's conscience.

Trust the genius Secretary of Defense, Robert McNamara, we were told, as well as the generals who told us repeatedly that they could see "the light at the end of the tunnel" as the war and the deaths dragged on week after week. After all, they have information we don't have. But trust was exactly what was lost. Never again would anyone from our generation trust the experts or the government. We were deceived and misled in a monumental way. Never again!

Like many young people at the time I wanted so badly to stop this insane war before anymore were killed or maimed. I helped organize an anti-war march through downtown Dubuque, Iowa; stood in a "silent vigil for peace" in front of the Federal Post Office with Joan Kiley and others each Sunday and did draft counseling. But the thing I had the most control over and perhaps the most meaningful was my own participation in the war.

It was a very big deal to defy the orthodoxy of the time and I struggled with it for many weeks. I knew my family and many others would have a problem with it but hoped they would eventually understand that it was paramount for me to follow my conscience.   If I were put in a situation where I either had to kill someone or be killed myself, surely my self-preservation would be triggered and I would kill. So the idea was to be true to my own inner moral code and to not put myself there in the first place.

A few months after my roommate, Tom, filed his CO claim I began working on my own. It was based similarly to his. I was a follower of Christ and as such was required to love and not to kill or injure. I felt strongly that I needed to be true to my faith and beliefs and that this was the right and moral thing to do. Some may have considered this cowardice or merely a way of getting out of fighting, but what they fail to realize is that the course of least resistance for many was to either enlist or be drafted. In some ways, it took much more effort and courage to choose to go against all the established forces in play and take a personal stand for peace, to go against the flow and say simply, "I won't go!"

I was assisted by the American Friends Service Committee, a Quaker organization with a long history of opposition to war and the establishment of peace through justice. As a Catholic it was more difficult to obtain Conscientious Objector (CO) status with your draft board, especially since the Catholic Church had developed what they called the Just War Theory, and, much to my dismay was virtually silent about what I considered an immoral and unjust war. So I worked hard to outline my personal beliefs and the compatibility of being a Catholic and also being a Conscientious Objector. In all it was a 10 page document with quotes from various bishops and Catholic teachers on the subject.

At the time I had no intention of ever needing to be classified a CO, since I was planning to continue my seminary studies on into graduate school (What was called the Theology part of my training). I simply wanted my position filed with the draft board as a statement of principle, knowing that they would not act on reclassifying me and drafting me unless I left the seminary and, therefore, lost my Divinity Student (4D) deferment.

I also mailed a copy of my request for CO status to my parents, hoping that after reading my carefully prepared statement they would, if not support, at least understand my position. I returned to Des Moines the following Christmas and, as was often the case, most of the relatives gathered at my Aunt Kay and Uncle Domo's house (they had the largest house in the family plus it had a partially finished basement).

After dinner my brother John approached me and said "Dad wants to see you in the basement." I was not prepared for what happened next.

He and my Uncle Floyd and later Jim Maloney were in the basement and he looked very upset. He immediately laid into me. "What's this bullshit about you being a Conscientious Objector," he shouted. "No son of mine is going to be a coward! I served my country and you should too," he added accusingly.

I was stunned and hurt. I tried to explain, "I'm perfectly willing to serve my country, just not as a soldier." (As a CO you were still required to put in two years of service. This could be either as a medic in the army or doing civilian service work). I made this clear in my application statement.

I was willing to serve my country, but I wasn't willing to kill for my country.

"Did you read the statement, because I made this clear there?" I said in defense, still shaken.

"No," he answered bluntly. The word hung in the air for a brief moment then pierced right through to my core. "No." It knocked me down, not to the floor, but down, down into a dark and despairing place. Here he was criticizing me and hadn't even taken the time to read it.

At the time, I didn't know how nor even felt it was right to stand up to my father. I did the only thing I could in the circumstances, I melted away and started balling uncontrollably. I was hurt deeply. I'm not sure which hurt more, being called a coward by my own father or his criticism of me without having the interest or decency to first read my statement.

I had sent it a few months before, so he'd had plenty of time to read it if he'd wanted to. It was obvious he didn't care enough about me to try to understand why I was taking this stand against war and violence. Perhaps subconsciously I had even hoped that he might admire me for it. I certainly didn't expect this kind of response.

Finally, my Uncle Floyd pushed back at him, "Lay off Joe. What the hell. You act like you're some great patriot. You know you hated being in the army!"

It wasn't exactly a ringing endorsement of my position, but I took it as a sympathetic voice in what was otherwise a very traumatic event. It also helped to wind down the confrontation and gave me a few minutes to compose myself before I climbed the stairs back up to the party. My face was red, my eyes swollen from all the crying and I could barely control the adrenaline induced shaking.

My father had a penchant for humiliating and excoriating others in public. I had witnessed it many times, often directed at my mother, and this was no exception. Though it took place in the basement, everyone knew at least generally what was going on. Of course, no one said a word and pretended as if nothing had happened. This only added to my humiliation. This incident more than any other created a gigantic rift between my father and me, on top of the rift caused by him trying to prevent me from going to a civil rights march earlier, and it took me many years before I could forgive him and to try to heal the relationship.

Many years later I was heartened to learn that many of my relatives present that day were actually very sympathetic to my cause and admired me for taking a principled stand against war. Of course, I had no idea at the time. What I remember feeling was very embarrassed and isolated for the rest of the afternoon.

Over time I also became more aware of just how big a deal it was to have a family member take this CO position. All my uncles had served in the army. In addition, my grandparents had immigrated from Italy in the early nineteen hundreds and felt a deep loyalty to America. They wanted desperately to blend into their new homeland. With the rise of Mussolini in World War II it became even more important for them to demonstrate their patriotism for their new country. We were not encouraged to learn or speak Italian, for example. Assimilation into the American culture and avoiding standing out was the overriding objective.

My father and most of the Italians on the south side of Des Moines grew up in this environment, so it was understandable that they would not want one of their own to show any signs of disloyalty. In addition, there was a desire to protect the family name and reputation. They were very concerned about what others thought of them and their family and thus, were very upset if a family member brought dishonor to their family. It wasn't uncommon to "disown" a family member who they thought had disgraced the family.

I can see now how this all played into my father's being upset with me. Nonetheless, it was a deeply painful and traumatic experience for me. In fact I did feel "disowned" by him in a way, or at the very least rejected.

THE BERRIGAN BROTHERS

Though I entered the seminary for a variety of reasons, some conscious, some not, I was now energized by a new concept of the priesthood, the concept of the activist priest. My role models were Father Dan Berrigan, a Jesuit Priest, and his brother Phil, a Josephite Priest. They were very active in the anti-war movement and were motivated by the belief that as Christians they must be a witness to the principles of Jesus.

They were known for breaking into draft board offices and throwing blood on the draft files, burning draft files with napalm, for hammering the heads of bombs (beating swords into plowshares), and other non-violent direct actions. In other words, they were my kind of priest. I wanted to be part of this movement, I wanted to change the world to a more peaceful loving place.

As a celibate priest I felt I would be in a perfect position to do civil disobedience when necessary, since I could go to jail and wouldn't have to worry about the effect on my family. I'd be freer to take a stand against injustice and war. I also hoped I could help change the Church for the better at the same time. I slowly saw my role as a revolutionary. I'd help change society and the Church for the better. I could contribute in both arenas. This would be my life's work.

I'M A SONGWRITER NOW

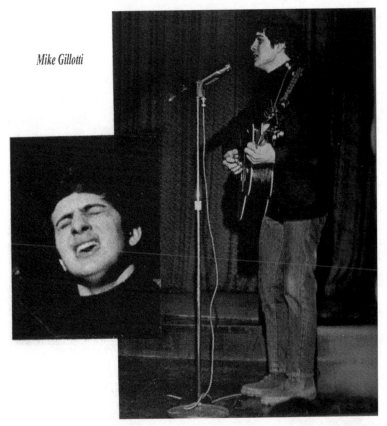

Mike Gillotti

Within a month after returning from summer camp in Colorado, my uncle Ernie bought me my first guitar. I didn't know the first thing about it and had to have John Ludwig or Paul tune it for me. They also showed me a few chords and I was off and running. Shortly, I wrote the first of many songs. I still have them in my songbook, but they're a little embarrassing now.

But back then I was inspired and loved this new vehicle of expression. Though I still could barely tune my guitar and only knew a few chords, I signed up for the student talent show. It was kind of a big deal and the college theater was filled with students and faculty. I remember standing on the right hand side of the stage in a navy blue sweater and Levis. A spotlight was shining on my face nearly blinding me and there were hundreds of people in the audience. I was nervous but tried to hide it.

I sang two original songs. One was called *The Innocent,* and was about the innocent civilians being killed in Vietnam. The room was silent. It was a magical experience. It's difficult to put in words, but it was like I became one with the audience and for the first time I felt I was communicating something important through my music and people were actually listening. I put my entire heart and soul into the performance and the applause was overwhelming. They were touched. I was hooked.

It wasn't long before I was playing guitar at masses at Loras and at St. Anthony's in Des Moines and at any other "sing-a-long" or jam that happened along.

THE OPPOSITE SEX

My involvement in extracurricular activities, namely the Big Brother Big Sister Program and the Buddy Club, brought me in regular contact with girls from Clark College. On Friday nights the Buddy Club would meet in Downtown Dubuque. Nobody had a car so we walked twenty or so blocks down Loras Blvd. to a community center. Here we would supervise developmentally disabled kids (at the time we called them retarded) who had gathered for an evening of socializing.

We students, half from Clark College and half from Loras, would help organize the activities and supervise the evening. Sometimes we'd show a movie, other times there was a dance. It was time well spent, I felt, and an unexpected benefit was I got really close to some of the Clark College girls. I found it very interesting and satisfying to have in depth conversations with them. Perhaps it was in part the fact that I was in the seminary and, therefore, they knew I wasn't interested in them in the same way other boys were. They felt safe with me. At any rate they confided in me and shared things with me that they couldn't or wouldn't share with their boyfriends. This struck me as very sad. I knew more about their inner thoughts and feelings than their own boyfriends did!

On the other hand it was an unexpected gift for me. I

began to see the opposite sex in an entirely different light. They became more real and more human and less and less fantasies or sexual objects. In the absence of the typical sexual tension between the sexes, I learned to be friends with them. I believe this experience helped me have more real and more meaningful relationships with women later in my life. This was one of many invaluable gifts I received from my time in the seminary.

THE BIG EASY

Since Dubuque was situated on the Mississippi River, some of the students found jobs cleaning out barges after the barges had emptied their loads of molasses, grains, coal, etc. Some had even worked on the barges as they made their way through the myriad of locks and dams all the way down to New Orleans. Randy, Jack O'Connor and I thought this would be a great adventure, sort of in the spirit of Huck Finn floating down the river on his raft.

However, because the barges moved so slowly and were further slowed by entering and exiting the locks and dams, the trip took nearly a week in one direction. We just could never find the time.

Still, the idea of traveling to New Orleans remained very appealing. We figured we'd have just enough time to hitchhike there and back during our Spring break junior year. As the time approached Randy backed out, so Jack and I decided to go on without him. Of course, neither of us had any money, so on a frosty March morning, we put our thumbs out along Highway 61, headed south.

That night we found ourselves freezing somewhere in Missouri. We walked across the highway and into a gas station to warm up. The attendant wasn't all that happy about it and after a few minutes said, "You guys are going to have to move on."

"But we're freezing," we pleaded.

"Sorry. You can't stay in here. My boss would be very unhappy." So we shivered out and back across the highway and waited for the rare car to pass. It must have been after midnight.

We had a classmate, Bob Essner, who lived in a small town south of St. Louis and he had told us we could stay at his house on the way down. We were desperate to reach there so we could thaw out and get some sleep, so against our better judgment took a ride with a car full of stoned, tripped out teens.

At one point the driver put on some psychedelic glasses that, because of the multiple beveled lenses, were impossible to see through. Jack and I were both mortified. I still don't know how he kept the car on the road. We reached our friends town sometime around 2:00 a.m., jumped out of the madman's car and made our way to Bob's house. As it turned out, Bob wasn't home, but his parents welcomed us in, gave us a place to sleep and breakfast in the morning.

We got lucky the next morning. We got picked up by a couple and their two children in a big Ford station wagon. "Where you heading?" he inquired.

"New Orleans," we responded.

"Jump in," he said, "that's exactly where we're going. We're coming back from a vacation in the Ozarks."

We were surprised the guy stopped since he had his

whole family with him. But such were the times. We were in the Age of Aquarius and love and understanding were in the air, along with the smell of Pachouli and marijuana. When we pulled into New Orleans he drove over to Jackson Square and said, "You guys wait in the car with my family. I'll be right back." He returned with a bag full of powdered donuts from Cafe' du Monde. What a great guy and what a great treat. And what a great way to enter THE BIG EASY! We'd made it!

Fortunately, Randy's friend, Art, lived in a frat house at Tulane University and we were able to crash there for free. We dined almost exclusively on 25 cents Burger King hamburgers. Our big splurge was a night out on Bourbon Street. We wandered off the main street and found a small club, where we listened to the most exquisite jazz trio I've ever heard. We met a couple of girls, but since we couldn't afford to buy them drinks, they eventually wandered off.

The evening culminated in the bar at the Top of The Mart, a rotating round room with panoramic views of the city and beyond. We were met outside the entrance by a host.

"You can't come in dressed like that," he said. "We require proper dress to enter. A sports coat is the minimum we'll allow."

"But we've come all the way down from Iowa. Can't you make an exception," I pleaded.

"No. Sorry. No exceptions."

Then Jack poured it on, "But you don't know what we

went through to get here. We almost froze to death. Can't you please let us in. We'll never make it down here again."

"All right," the host relented, "follow me."

He led us into a back room near the entrance, where several sports coats of various sizes and colors were hanging against the back wall. He handed us each a poorly fitting coat and opened the door to the bar.

They also required that you buy a drink if you wanted to stay. Drinks were around a buck each and it nearly busted us. After paying such an exorbitant price we were determined to "ride" the revolving room the full 360 degrees. This took around an hour, so we sipped our first and only drink very, very slowly. We were afraid if our glasses went empty, we would be asked to leave.

Neither of us had ever experienced anything like this before. The room crept around at a snail's pace and you could see for miles in all directions. First New Orleans itself came into view, then the delta of the Mississippi River where the river dumped its water and silt into the Gulf of Mexico, until finally we were back where we'd started. What a trip!

The following day we visited the above ground cemetery. We learned that they had to bury people above ground because New Orleans was below sea level. Apparently, in the past at high tide, caskets would pop out of their grave-sites and float around the city. As you can imagine, this freaked everyone out, so they eventually created these unique, above ground cemeteries.

Some of the tombs were small little houses scattered inside the walls of the cemetery. Others, presumably those of the poor, were in what looked like huge drawers positioned all along the inside walls. It reminded me of a giant chest of draws with bodies instead of clothes stacked several levels high. I imagined that they simply slid the body in and then slid the drawer closed. It was all very spooky so we got out of there quickly after checking it out.

Riding the trolley down St. Charles St. and back to Tulane University, we packed up our things for the trip upstream to Dubuque. After finding our way back to Highway 61, we put our thumbs out pointing north. The return trip was a blur. I do remember Mrs. Essner putting us up again in Missouri, but little else. We arrived in Dubuque less than a week after we left. Don't ask me how we did it, but we traveled 1100 miles each way and spent a total of $11.00 each, a world record held since 1969!

YOU'RE TOO SERIOUS

One evening I was walking down Loras Boulevard with Linda Bisignano, who was attending Clark College. Her older brother was in the major (graduate) seminary, St. Bernard's, just outside Dubuque. I was going on about the brutality of the Vietnam War, the hatred and bigotry directed toward blacks, the injustice of poverty and how the government had deceived us and had not lived up to the principles of our great nation.

She interrupted stating: "You and my brother are so alike. You're both just too serious."

I was offended and reacted immediately. "These are serious times requiring serious thought and action. How dare you criticize me for being too serious. Maybe you need to be less frivolous and stop partying all the time."

Looking back now, of course, she was right. I couldn't remember the last time I really laughed or let myself have a good time. There was an unspoken belief that while others were suffering, it was not ok to feel good or have fun. We were to feel their suffering and to suffer ourselves if we were to live according to Jesus's principles. After all Christ suffered during his torturing and crucifixion. Were we not to follow his example? Self-flagellation anyone?

This attitude played out in my own neighborhood as I was growing up. Neighbors and relatives would identify with the suffering Christ and take on an identity of the sufferer.

Suffering was desirable and honorable and we were to wear it like a badge. Though it was often a play for sympathy, it was also simply their way of being in the world. Like me, they just couldn't allow themselves to feel good.

I believe it was Abraham Lincoln who said, ". . . folks are pretty much as happy as they decide they'll be." I later came to see that the creator didn't put us here to be miserable, but rather to be happy and fulfilled. It's really okay to be happy!

Chapter IV

THE BEGINNING OF THE END

During Christmas break my senior year I called an old girlfriend, Linda O. I had been curious about marijuana but hadn't tried it yet. I knew she had. She invited me over to her cousin's house on the east side of Des Moines. Her cousin was staying in her parent's basement and as I entered the room, I was open to whatever they offered me. I figured it was a safe environment for my first experience.

Linda put on the newly released Beatles, Abbey Road album and lit up a joint. I didn't feel anything at first, but after a few minutes I was higher than a kite. The music was flowing all over me and through me. It was the most beautiful sound I'd ever heard. All my senses were heightened and I laughed uncontrollably. What an amazing experience!

After a while my mood shifted. All three of us were lying on the bed talking and laughing. Suddenly I became convinced that they were both trying to seduce me. We'd been warned about this in the seminary. There were certain women who considered it a challenge to woo you away from the priesthood. Linda rolled over toward me and her leg met mine. I froze. All I could think about now was how I could make myself come down and get the hell out of there.

To make matters worse, when one of them began to

speak, I would hear the first part of the sentence but not the end. The end just trailed off, unintelligibly, the words and their meaning lost. As a result I was certain they were talking about me and plotting ways to seduce me. The whole experience had gone terribly sour.

Afraid to reveal to them my thoughts and feelings, I instead focused on when the marijuana would wear off. "How long does this last?" I quizzed. "When will I come down?"

"It's hard to say," Linda responded. She was surprised at the question but it was obvious they both saw how anxious I was. I think they felt responsible. They tried to calm me down, but it wasn't working. I was flipping out. In fact every time one of them spoke it only fueled my paranoia.

I got up abruptly and, in a troubled and dazed state, made my way to my father's car. I prayed I still had the capacity to drive it home safely. I was so distracted that I soon turned down a one-way street, going against the traffic. Now I was in a full panic.

I somehow managed to turn around and find my way home, only to be certain that my parents would know immediately I was in an altered state. I tried to act cool as I walked through the living room and up the stairs to my bedroom. I collapsed into bed in a high state of stress.

The next morning I woke up and was still high. Now I was really worried. What had I done. What if I NEVER come down! I was so unfamiliar with this drug that I truly was concerned that it might have a permanent effect, that I had opened up a door to my mind that I wouldn't be able to close again.

That afternoon I was still high and still frightened. I decided to call Linda for some reassurance and to confront her for trying to seduce me. She was shocked that I was still high and tried to assure me that I'd come down soon. She was also shocked that I thought they were trying to seduce me. No way, she said. I argued with her and called her a liar. "I know you were, Linda!"

"No I wasn't, I swear." I was absolutely convinced that she had and was angry at her for lying to me.

I met with her the next day outside Tersi's clothing store on S.W. 9th St., remarkably still high. I asked her to her face, "Were you and your cousin trying to seduce me?"

"No, of course not," she answered. "I respect that you're in the seminary and would never do that."

Finally, I had to accept that she was telling the truth and that it was "all in my head." This is what paranoia looks like. I'd had a direct experience of it and it really troubled me. To be so convinced in my own mind that something was so that wasn't so at all!! Wow, what an experience and what a lesson.

I had now been celibate for nearly four years and felt I was really handling it quite well. I wasn't walking around frustrated or horny. I hardly ever masturbated, and, when I did no longer felt it was necessary to confess it as a sin. I decided a little release now and then was probably ok, just so long as it was very rare.

Plus, unlike some of my classmates, I knew what I was giving up. This gave me confidence that I had somehow mastered this very challenging psychological role. Now, after this incident, I wasn't so sure that I was as mentally healthy as I thought. The window to my subconscious had been cracked open slightly and it pointed to some malfunctioning machinery inside. I didn't like what I saw but just couldn't deal with it. So I closed the window quickly and got on with the work of preparing myself for the priesthood.

Back at Loras I was now part of the small inner circle of students who got stoned. It was our own little secret. There was another good reason to keep it secret. It was illegal and likely would result in our suspension or dismissal from college if we were caught. We winked knowingly to each other when other students would look at us quizzically during weekend parties or events.

At one party off campus I got stoned and was soon dancing with Karen B. All of my feelings and senses were heightened and aroused, as well as other things of a private nature. Normally I would resist these feelings, but tonight, feeling Karen's body next to mine as we danced, I surrendered and let nature take its course.

The next thing I remember we were in my room in Rohlman Hall (the Seminary dorm) making out on my bed. Our clothes stayed on but I was still transported to another realm.

The following day, after my feet were on the ground, I felt some regret and struggled with what had happened the night before. Though I tried to deny it and put the whole thing out of my head, I couldn't deny how good it felt. I didn't know it then, or perhaps didn't want to admit it, but this, together with my experience with Linda, was the beginning of the end for me and the priesthood.

THE FIRST DRAFT LOTTERY

During the final semester at Loras I made a decision to give up my seminarian deferment (4 D) and allow myself to be drafted, intending to do my two years of service as a Non-Combatant Conscientious Objector. In an effort to make the draft more fair, Nixon instituted a lottery system in 1970. I was in the very first lottery. My birthday, March 17, drew number 33. I believe everyone with numbers up to 150 or so was drafted.

I was happy to get the low number in a way. I had decided that I didn't want to become a special privileged priest with a special deferment. I wanted to be treated like everyone else and have to deal with the war and draft just like everyone else my age. I didn't want to place myself above anyone, but rather be among them, one of them.

I knew the risks involved. Although I had filed for CO status with my draft board, they wouldn't act on the request until I was eligible for the draft. I knew then, that if I weren't granted CO status, I would go to prison before I'd allow myself to be drafted into the army and put in a position of either killing or being killed. I was also clear I wouldn't escape to Canada as some of my classmates planned to do. I would stay here and take a stand for non-violence and for ending the war. My own conscience demanded it, and who knows, maybe it would also have an effect on others attitudes about war and violence. Just maybe.

I had a meeting with Bishop Dingman in Des Moines just before graduation. We met at an International Pancake House on Ingersoll Ave. I was a bit nervous being alone with the bishop, but he was gracious and put me at ease.

"I want to let you know that I'm planning to move to San Francisco right after graduation. In my mind I'm not really leaving the seminary. I see this move as a continuation of my studies. It won't be in a formal seminary but rather in the Seminary of The World."

"Normally," he shared, "I would try to dissuade you. Nearly everyone who tries something like this does not return to their seminary training. But I can see you are determined."

"I am. I think it will make me a better priest if I have to live in the world for a while, get a job, pay rent, and deal with all the issues that regular people have to deal with. In addition, I plan to live in one of the black districts of the city, The Fillmore. This I feel, will give me a better understanding of their suffering and put me in a better position to help them and the cause of civil rights when I become a priest."

"I respect your intention and your desire to be the best priest you can. But, of course, I will have to take you off the roles of the seminary and thus, you will be subject to the military draft."

"I understand. I even welcome it. I don't want to be a special privileged priest. I want to have to deal with the war and draft just like everyone else my age. I'll do my two years of Alternative Service and then go on to graduate school in Theology and pick up where I left off."

"I wish you luck," he said in parting. I could tell he wasn't that crazy about what I was doing and feared he'd lose another seminarian. I wasn't worried. I knew I would return. I was still very committed to becoming a priest. This plan made perfect sense to me. And besides I could go be a hippy for a couple years on the west coast! We shook hands and both went our ways.

WHAT HAPPENS IN VEGAS,
ONLY MY BROTHER KNOWS

During this period of our lives Randy and I were still bound together by our insatiable need for adventure. The latest one, and likely our last as college students, was to hitch hike to Las Vegas during Spring break and visit my brother Sam, who had moved there a couple years earlier. We took off from Dubuque on a chilly March morning with a few dollars in our pockets, some old boy scout packs and very thin cotton sleeping bags.

Later that day we were dropped at an exit ramp on the Kansas Turnpike. Within minutes a state trooper pulled over and arrested us for hitchhiking on the turnpike. "We didn't see any signs, officer." I argued.

"There are signs all along the turnpike." he answered.

"Well, we didn't see any, and we were looking for one," I continued. "This isn't right."

Randy tried to get me to shut up, worrying I was only making things worse.

"Get in the car," the trooper commanded. "It's too late to take you before the judge, so you'll have to spend the night in the Sedgewedge County Jail."

We continued to profess our innocence all the way to the jail, to no avail.

We were booked into the jail and put into a holding cell with a couple other "criminals."

One of them was a teenage kid who'd been arrested for stealing a car. He strutted around the cell swearing and kicking at the bars. He was a real tough son-of-a bitch and we were a little anxious about being in the same cell with him. A short time later the kid got a phone call that his mother had died while he was away. He sat down and balled like a baby. "Some tough guy," Randy said under his breath.

Next we had to surrender our clothes for blue overhauls, were each handed a mattress and a blanket and led to our cell. Randy asked the guard if we could "room together." We were both happy that his request had been granted.

The first thing that struck me was the noise and chaos. There must have been ten radios blaring, all on different stations. There was also a lot of talking between the cells and a pay phone was being wheeled down the hall, stopping in front of each cell so calls could be made through the bars. Other prisoners further down the cellblock were yelling to hurry up and get off the phone so they could have their turn. It was all very crazy.

Our biggest worry was that we'd be detained so long or be fined so high (we only had about $20 each on us) that we'd have to abort our trip. Our break was only a week long.

Trying to look on the positive side, we did have a mattress and a place to sleep that night rather than camping on the side of the road somewhere.

The next day we were taken before the judge and quickly realized we weren't the only ones caught up in this "hitch-hiking trap." There were several very hippie looking kids sitting next to us and acting very belligerently. It was "fuck this" and "fuck the judge" etc. We tried to move our chairs as far away from them as possible, fearful the judge would think we were traveling together.

There just happened to be an attorney sitting near us. I assumed he'd heard about the big busts the night before and came down for some courtroom entertainment. He was kind enough to advise us that if we pled not guilty, the judge would assign a court date and we'd have to return for it. So even though we felt deeply that justice was not being served, we reluctantly pled guilty. Our hearts dropped when the judge fined us $10 each and then rose again when he suspended the fines.

No way were we going to risk returning to the turnpike to resume our hitchhiking. One of the clerks directed us to a two-lane highway just west of town. Randy remembered that a Kansas State student, Danielle, had dropped us on the turnpike and he had her phone number. We called her from the lobby to see if she could help us out. She was sympathetic but had nothing more to offer. We assumed she didn't want to be seen associating with two ex-cons! Somehow we managed to get to the two-lane highway headed West and stuck out our thumbs.

We knew most of the traffic heading west would be traveling on the turnpike, so expected that it would likely take us a long time to get a ride here. It turned out to be even worse than we thought. Only one car passed by every half hour or so. We stood there forever, cursing our bad luck and despairing of ever getting out of Kansas. Then Craig, a Vietnam vet. pulled over. We both saw the open case of beer in the back seat but at that point felt we had no choice but to get in.

As we drove westward, he continued to consume cans of beer. By the time he stopped at a bar and pool hall somewhere near the Arizona border, he was totally intoxicated. Randy started playing pool with him and he kept ordering whiskeys. We were totally stressed and since we were in the middle of nowhere, knew we had to get back in the car with him after the pool game. Fearing for our lives, we hit upon a plan.

"While I distract him at the pool table, you sneak up behind him and take a big drink from his whiskey glass," Randy whispered. We had both noticed that he would set his glass down on the edge of the pool table every time he took a shot.

"But what if he sees me?" I worried.

"Just do it," Randy shot back, quietly. "We don't have any choice. He could kill both of us."

"All right, all right," I whispered back. "I don't really like this plan, and I don't really like whiskey, but I'll try."

So whenever he took a shot that wasn't facing his whiskey

glass, I quietly walked up and took a big gulp. He'd finish off the glass and then order another one, but at least we cut his actual consumption in half.

This went on for a couple more refills when finally Craig slurred, "Let's get ou-out a here."

As we walked to the car Craig and I were laughing and giggling. He and I were a little wobbly. We were both having a great time and continued to as we drove off. Randy was not amused. He later confided that he promised God that if he would get us out of this situation safely, he would return to the seminary (he had dropped out a couple years before) and never think of sex or women again.

Thankfully, his prayers were answered when Craig pulled over at a roadside motel, opened his car door and immediately fell out onto the parking lot. We dragged him into a room. We both agreed we had tempted fate long enough. The next morning we got up early and started hitchhiking while he was still sleeping. We prayed someone would pick us up before he awoke and spotted us, fearing we would feel "obligated" to get back in the car with him. We wouldn't want to make him feel bad.

We ended up on a freeway ramp outside of Flagstaff, Arizona late at night. No one was stopping and we were beat, so we jumped a fence and set up a pup tent in the woods just out of sight from the interstate. We noticed scattered areas of snow on the ground but didn't give it too much thought. But when the sun was well down the temperature dropped precipitously. We started a campfire but it barely kept the front of our bodies warm. Our backs were freezing.

We crawled into our sleeping bags but I began shivering so badly I couldn't sleep. I crawled out and stirred up the fire and spent the most miserable night of my life shaking uncontrollably, smoke burning my eyes with every shift of the wind. I could not get warm and I could not sleep. I wondered if this was what purgatory was like. You're neither in heaven nor in hell, and wondered why I was being punished so much. I thought studying for the priesthood came with some immunity to this kind of suffering. Randy, on the other hand, had a better, thicker sleeping bag and was sound asleep while I hovered around the fire all night long.

The next morning we hitched a ride in a VW Bug to the south rim of the Grand Canyon. It was so magnificent and beautiful that I nearly forgot the misery of the previous night.

I couldn't help noticing that there was a sleeping bag bunched up in the back seat. I'd never seen one quite like it before. It was very fluffy and flexible, unlike my conventional bag that you rolled up tightly to carry.

"It's a down sleeping bag," the driver told me.

"I've never heard of it before. What is it?" I inquired.

"It's not like the other bags," he said. "They stuff goose down in between the bag's panels."

After what I went through last night, I was all ears. "Does it work in the winter?"

"Yes," the driver responded. "If you have enough feathers it will work in below zero temperatures."

"It's so light," I said to Randy. "I don't see how it could work."

"Oh, it works," the driver interjected. "Trust me. It keeps you toasty."

It made me sick with envy to hear this. I vowed it would be my very next purchase.

That night we landed at my brother Sam's apartment in Vegas thankful we were still alive. We had survived the drunk driver and the frozen Arizona tundra. Sam was the first in our family to really break out of Des Moines and was working as a draftsman and enjoying life out West. He had even bought himself a motorcycle and, given the weather, drove it almost exclusively. Even so, I was still totally shocked and grateful when as we were about to leave, he offered to give me his car to drive back home. "I don't need it," he said. "I've got my motorcycle."

It was a 1960 red Anglia, better known as an English Ford. He did have some concerns about the car making it back to Iowa, however, and knowing we had no money, he gave us his credit card just in case. I refused to take it but he insisted. He said I could mail it back to him once we were home safely. He had to look after his younger brother.

Not only was my brother the most generous person in the world, he was, I learned, also very psychic. A hundred miles south of Salt Lake City the generator stopped working. With the red generator light on we knew we were in trouble and that the car would stop dead as soon as the battery was drained. We limped into the small town of Beaver and to a garage, but the mechanic said he didn't have a replacement part on hand. He'd have it shipped down on a Greyhound bus the next day from Salt Lake City. We'd have to spend the night. There was only one hotel in town and it was horrible but cheap. I believe we even had to share the same bed.

As we're standing in his shop working this all out, I notice a Book Of Mormon on the counter. "What's this book?" I inquired.

"It's the Mormon scripture," He answered, "Kind of like your Bible. Joseph Smith wrote it down from the golden tablets the Angel Moroni gave him."

I could tell he was subtly trying to convert us and neither Randy or I were interested. He did get our attention, though, when he offered, "I'm a member of the church. In fact I'm a bishop in the church."

We stared in disbelief. A bishop. We both looked at the Book of Mormon on the counter and then to this man in coveralls and greasy hands. We just couldn't get our heads around it. Having been through 16 years of Catholic schools including the seminary we knew what bishops looked like and what they did for a living, and they certainly didn't look like or work as mechanics. What kind of weird church could this be?

"You should stop in Salt Lake City on your way home. I think you'd find Mormon Square very interesting and you could learn more about the church," he suggested.

Thanks to Sam's MasterCard we were on our way the next

day and, in fact, did stop briefly in Salt Lake. We wandered through Mormon Square and the information building. We learned about Joseph Smith being given golden tablets from the Angel Moroni. There was also some kind of pictorial about American Indians showing their relationship to the lost tribe of Israel. It was all very strange but interesting.

We stood in the back of the hall of the Mormon Tabernacle Choir and listened closely as a pin was dropped in the front of the room. We could hear it clearly all the way in the back. Amazing acoustics.

Next we walked over to the Mormon Temple (it looked like a cathedral to me) but were told we could not go inside.

"Why not?" I asked the staff person.

"You can't go in because you wouldn't be able to handle it," he responded.

"Why wouldn't I be able to handle it. What's in there?"

"I can't really talk about it. You're not even a member, for one thing," he answered.

Since that day I've been intrigued by what's inside that temple that I wouldn't be able to handle. Now I finally know. They were hiding Mitt Romney in there!

As we neared Cheyenne the windows were frosting over and our legs were freezing. The heater couldn't keep up with the outside temperature. Randy and I argued heatedly about whether to stop for the night. I was concerned about the car breaking down again. We'd been driving for something like 16 hours straight. He wanted to get back to his girlfriend in Iowa. I overruled him and he was angry at me the rest of the trip.

We pulled off the freeway and got the cheapest room we could find. Not only did we get some rest, it was also a chance to warm up before we got back on the road. We spent the next night in Des Moines, then it was back to Loras College to finish up our last semester of college / seminary.

In a wink we were about to begin our graduation weekend. My parents and two younger sisters drove up to Dubuque. At the reception the night before the commencement ceremony I introduced my father to my favorite history professor, Dr. Auge. He immediately tore into him. "So you're the one giving my son all these radical ideas! You're the one who's been brain washing my son!"

"No," Dr. Auge responded. "I'm not giving him any ideas. He's simply responding to all the violence and injustice around us."

My dad wasn't buying it and kept on him, "He wasn't like this before he came up here. He was a good Catholic boy. Now he's different. You've turned him into a radical."

I was so angry and embarrassed and in a rare moment of courage stood up to my father. "I didn't appreciate you insulting my professor like that." I said angrily.

"I didn't insult anybody. And don't you talk to me that way young man!" he threatened.

Obviously this didn't go over well with my dad. The next day he told my mother that he would not attend the graduation ceremony. He felt I had been disrespectful to him and no way was he going to show up. She was horrified and begged him to reconsider.

In the end he did come and I believe he was very proud to witness his youngest son graduate with "magna cum laude" honors. Though my two older brothers had attended college, I was the first in our family to actually graduate.

If only I could have left it at that. Several of us had decided before hand to turn the graduation ceremony into a protest against the Vietnam War. We wore black arm bands under our gowns and raised our arms in the air as we walked up to get our diplomas.

Chapter V

IF YOU'RE GOING TO SAN FRANCISCO, BE SURE TO WEAR SOME FLOWERS IN YOUR HAIR

In Front of our Dolores St. flat. My room's on the second floor corner

I had heard the song, *If You're Going to San Francisco* ..., and had seen the newscasts about life in the Haight and Asbury. There were people there trying to live an alternative lifestyle, where money, power and success were no longer the goal of life. In this "new way of living" what was important was loving relationships with others, inner peace, creative expression, fulfillment, and of course, peace in the world. No more wars and violence. Make love and not war was the theme.

This all resonated with my heart's desire. And what a great experience it would be to kill two birds with one stone: to fulfill my two year CO requirement while at the same time to experience living on the West Coast in the hippie capital of San Francisco.

Within a week of graduation in June of 1970, I was loading my little red Anglia with a suitcase, guitar and sleeping bag. A couple girls from Dubuque, Mary and Susan, needed a ride and as soon as they got to Des Moines we took off for San Francisco. I had $50 in my pocket. The girls had even less between them. Worried about being busted for pot and ruining the whole trip, I told the girls they could not bring any marijuana with them on the trip. They agreed.

No one thought the Anglia would make it all the way to the West Coast, but I wasn't worried. The backup plan was, if it broke down, we'd simply abandon it on the spot and hitchhike the rest of the way. I'd already had so much hitch-hiking under my belt that I was confident we'd get there just fine.

Mary's brother lived in San Francisco and I had a friend there, the vice rector of the seminary, Father Ede, who was studying for his PhD. in Berkeley. He had offered to put me up until I got settled.

We managed to get into New Mexico the first day after

over 16 hours of driving. Fortunately for us the car hadn't blown up yet either. Wanting to conserve the little money we had, I dropped off the girls a block from a rundown motel and checked in by myself. Then I went back and picked them up and we all snuck into the room. As I closed the door, I noticed the owner was watching through the office window. I worried all night that he'd throw us out, but he never did.

I soon learned that my fellow passengers were not as sweet and innocent as I thought. We stopped for food at a local store, and when we returned to the car, they pulled out some cokes and chips they'd hidden under their jackets. I was ok with cheating the motel, but this was completely unacceptable and shocking to me. I was a cheat but I sure as hell was not a thief!

Later in the day we stopped at a gas station. They both came out of the restroom with smiles on their faces and reeking of marijuana.

"What the hell is this?" I asked angrily. "You agreed not to bring any marijuana with you on this trip."

"Why you getting so uptight, man?" Susan said. "You need to be cool and not worry so much."

"That's easy for you to say. It's my car and it could screw up the whole trip if we get pulled over by the cops."

"Don't worry, don't worry," Mary added, "Everything's groovy, man. Relax."

"Screw you."

"We won't do it anymore," promised Susan. "We don't have any left anyway. We smoked it all up."

They were lying. Every time after this that we stopped for gas I could clearly smell it. They tried to disguise it with Pachouli Oil but it wasn't working. I was really pissed, both for them not taking my concerns seriously and then for lying to me afterward. I couldn't wait to get to San Francisco and get rid of both of them.

My brother Sam's apartment in Las Vegas was our next stop. We slept for only a few hours and then, as was the common wisdom, we departed at midnight to avoid the daytime desert heat. It's not that we were particularly concerned about our own discomfort. It was the car we were worried about. Older cars tended to overheat in the desert. In fact, as an added precaution, I removed the thermostat from the top of the radiator. This was also a common practice back then. It allowed more water to flow through the radiator and engine block and reduced the odds of it overheating.

Up until then I'd been doing all the driving, but as we approached Los Angeles I was nearly asleep at the wheel. One of the girls said she could drive a stick, and I gladly turned the car over to her. Every time she let the clutch out, she killed the engine, which, in turn killed my confidence in her driving skills. So after an hour or so, I took control of the driving and kept it the rest of the way.

I had never seen an ocean before in my life. We don't have them in Iowa. When we pulled off just north of LA for our first one on one experience, I was overwhelmed. The Pacific Ocean, how immense and how beautiful! I was also struck by the constant sound of the waves roaring. I hadn't expected it to be so incessant or so loud. I could have stayed there all day and just soaked it in, but we had to move on to the north.

STARTING ANEW

As we approached San Francisco, Mary told me she had directions to her brother's house. She directed me off Highway 101 and we immediately got lost. By this point I was deeply exhausted and my nerves were frayed. It didn't help that we were going up and then down the steepest hills I'd ever driven on in my life and I was stressed out. First I thought the engine was going to blow as it strained to climb up. Then on the way down I was sure that the brakes would give out. I was ready to kill her. We somehow managed to find her brother's flat near Castro and Market. We said our goodbyes and said we should keep in touch, but I didn't mean it. I didn't care if I never saw them again.

I then fumbled my way to Funston Blvd. near Golden Gate Park to where Father Ede was waiting. He was generous to offer me an extra room in a house he was staying at. He rented a room on the second floor of an old house from a one armed Spanish lady. I found out later she wasn't all that thrilled when my stay evolved from one week to two and then three. I was working hard to find a job that would qualify as Alternative Service and didn't want to move until I knew where I'd be working. I had even applied for a job in Berkeley, so wanted to see if I got the job, in which case I'd move across the bay.

I was joined on the second floor by another priest, Father Bill, whom I thought was just visiting the area for a while. I learned shortly that he was one of many priests who were abandoning the priesthood during this period. There was a mass exit and for many reasons, not the least of which was the requirement of celibacy.

I found it ironic that he and many others were leaving at the exact time that I was going into it. Father Ede and he were acutely aware of this irony and as a result, never said anything that might discourage me from continuing. They were also very supportive, taking me on "orientation" rides to Twin Peaks and other areas of the city so I'd be able to find my way around. Frequently they would take me out to dinner and picked up the tab. I could tell they were worried about me and my survival. I wasn't. I was confident and in retrospect, naively optimistic.

As I said, after a couple weeks the one armed widow let Father Ede know that I was out staying my welcome. Luckily I found a job in Ghirardelli Square working at the non-profit International Children's Art Center. I was basically a janitor and classroom assistant and made $150 a month. My predecessor was also a C.O., so all the paper work had been worked out to qualify the position as Alternative Service.

I took the job before I'd actually received CO status from my draft board back in Des Moines and was disappointed when they rejected my claim and demanded I come back to Des Moines to testify before them. Not having the money to make the trip and not wanting to lose my job, I asked my former neighbor and one of the references on my application, John Tapscott, to testify for me. Soon after I was granted CO status.

I've always felt a deep gratitude to him for doing this for me. If he hadn't, my life would have taken a dramatic turn, since I likely would have been sent to prison. There was no way I was going into the Army or to Vietnam. I found out later that my father and uncle and many others on the south side were very upset with him for supporting me with this. They all saw conscientious objection as unpatriotic and faulted him for enabling it.

I loved the job. There was a gallery of children's art from all over the world in the front and a classroom in the back. On weekends we'd put a bunch of wood blocks and Elmer's glue on a large table out in the courtyard and let young children express their creativity. It really didn't matter what their art piece looked like. It was the act of creating that was what we were after.

In the afternoons there were art classes in the back and each day I'd eat my lunch down by the bay ("sittin on the dock of the bay") and look out at the Golden Gate Bridge. What an amazing work of art it is. I had to pinch myself. Was I really in San Francisco! It was all so new and exhilarating.

Staying true to my mission to prepare myself to be the best possible priest, I rented a room in the Fillmore District and began tutoring at Sacred Heart School nearby. It was one of the poorest black areas in the city and I was intentionally there to educate myself to their plight. Everything was coming together just as I had imagined it would. I was so happy and high from it all.

My room was small and overlooked Fillmore Street. It had a small refrigerator and a hot plate, a sink and a single bed. I shared the bathroom with the second floor tenants. To create a couch, I took the mattress off the bed and folded it, shoving one half against the wall and leaving the second half on the floor. I then slept on the box springs. My rent was $65 a month. I was a hippie now, or as I later referred to myself, a "quasi-hippie."

I let my hair grow long until it closely resembled Bob Dylan's. I bought a second hand pair of Levis at Goodwill, cut the seams at the end of the legs and sewed in narrow triangles of leather. This resulted in what I thought was the coolest pair of bell bottoms. I also wore my cowboy boots as much as possible.

Though I had missed the Renaissance period of Haight and Ashbury by a couple years, there were still many communal households and hippie countercultural folks inhabiting the city. I definitely gravitated to them and their lifestyle. We were going to change the world. No more greedy capitalism. No more war. No more hatred and bigotry. We'd fill the world with love and peace and justice. It would envelope the world and change everything. I was so happy to be part of this!

This was also the period of the "sexual revolution" and it seemed like everyone in San Francisco was having tons of sex except me. All the old rules about being married before having sex were out the window. I'd been celibate for four years and now I naively thought that having sex with an "old lady" along with all the other experiences, would make me a better priest. After all, if I was to counsel couples, it behooved me to know what this was all about. It also bothered me that though I had had sexual experiences with women during high school, I had not gone "all the way" with one. I was what the church called a "technical virgin." I had not had intercourse.

Remarkably, I thought at the time that I could have a live-in girlfriend and then after two years tell her that I was sorry I hadn't mentioned it before, but I was actually studying to be a priest and would have to leave now. What an idiotic idea. And how unfair to my partner. Fortunately, this fantasy relationship never really materialized. Not that I didn't try.

Another reason I did not tell anyone that I was still preparing for the priesthood was that as soon as others knew, they would begin treating me differently than they treated others.

Some would treat me with more deference, some were more careful about their language and swearing. Others, especially in San Francisco, might think I was crazy to be doing something like this. I didn't want that. I wanted to be treated like anyone else. This, I thought would also help me with my own self-identity and image. How would I ever know who I really am if everyone treated me as someone different or special? I wanted to know who I was as a person and not as a priest in training.

This deception was thorough. My friends didn't know. My employers didn't know. My co-workers didn't know. And certainly my prospective girlfriends didn't know. I simply told them I had graduated from college in Iowa as a History major and that was it. I was living a big lie and it would later come back to haunt me.

A ROBBERY ON FILLMORE STREET

The Fillmore was a dangerous place. Frequently I would hear gunshots in the evening. Many of the corners were occupied by prostitutes, their pimps not far away. Black men stood on the corners near vacant lots, drinking from brown paper bags and looking very annoyed when I walked by. They seemed to resent a white boy living in their neighborhood.

I was never really frightened for my safety until one day while I was walking home down Fillmore Street, a young, teenage boy walked up beside me, put a knife in my side and said, "Give me your money!"

I had been reading and thinking about Gandhi and Martin Luther King Jr. and their adoption of non-violence in their respective struggles for justice and equality. On a personal level, when confronted by a violent person, Gandhi had written that the two most common reactions were either fear or anger. If you reacted in either of these ways you were very likely to escalate the violence. If you display neither of these, he claimed, if you stayed calm and neutral, you could "disarm" your opponent.

Although I was frightened by this young man's knife in my side, I didn't show it. Instead, I kept walking and said, somewhat annoyed, "Look, I'm late and I have to get home."

The teenager paused for a moment, taken back. Then he repeated, "Give me your money," and added, "Or I'm gonna cut you!"

Somehow I stayed calm, and didn't make eye contact. "Look, I really need to get home," I said, and kept walking.

I held my breath for a several more steps, prepared to feel some cold steel in my side. Finally I looked around and he was nowhere to be found.

When I returned to my room, I started to shake uncontrollably as the reality of what just happened and what could have happened hit me. At the same time I was overjoyed that my non-violent response had worked, just as Gandhi had predicted! I was from that moment on even more committed to non-violent action. I had just proved that it works!

FORT HELP

Dr. Joel Fort had written a timely book titled, *The Pleasure Seekers*, in the late sixties. It became a hit with the counterculture because, among other things, he pointed out the hypocrisy of outlawing marijuana while alcohol was perfectly legal. He also noted that alcohol was much more dangerous to one's health than marijuana. Building on his super star status he decided to open a clinic in an old warehouse south of Market Street. It was to be called, what else but, Fort Help, the Center for Special Social and Sexual Problems.

When I arrived they were still putting up the walls and sheet rock, so I jumped right in. Not wanting to be too conventional, all the walls were curved, making the building of them and the sheet rocking more difficult and time consuming and delaying the opening. One day while I was working on a step ladder, a middle-aged woman in a short skirt came in. She said hello and was a little flirtatious. "How you doing, cutie," she said as she passed by. "What's your name?"

"I'm Michael. What's yours?"

"I'm Charlene," she said, "I'm one of the counselors."

"We'll I'm just helping finish this sheetrock so you'll have a room to do your work in. I'll be volunteering as a Greeter."

The next day we were all sitting around in a circle on folding chairs having a staff meeting and introductions. I just happened to sit next to Charlene. When it was her turn to share, something in her voice caught my attention. It seemed a little deeper than it should have been. As she spoke it slowly dawned on me. She's not a woman! SHE'S A MAN!

She made it clear she was not a transvestite. That's simply a man who likes to wear women's clothing. So what was she? I learned that she was a transsexual and was preparing to have surgery to remove her penis and create a vagina. Because it was not reversible, they had to go through a thorough evaluation and waiting period. I tried very hard to act as if this was no big deal, but I'm sure everyone in the room saw my mind spinning in disbelief.

Before the mud on the walls was dry and with only a few walls painted, I found myself volunteering as a "Greeter" just inside the front door. My job was to direct clients to the right practitioner and to assist in the methadone program for heroin addicts. Even though the place was chaotic and unfinished, I loved working there and meeting all these interesting clients and staff, and, most of all, feeling I was doing something of service and something useful.

Whenever I had an opportunity to visit with an addict as they came in for their methadone dose, I would probe them about why they got started, how and why they got addicted. I was expecting some grand explanation about how they wanted to escape the world and all its suffering, but most of them had no idea. All they knew was that they were seriously under the command and spell of this drug.

One of the clients, Jim, shared, "I used to get high from it. It was a rush, kind of like an orgasm. But now I just use it to keep from getting sick. I don't want to go through withdrawal. It's a bitch."

"Why did you start," I asked.

"I don't know. A friend turned me onto it, that's all I know."

He then went up to the counter and got his paper cup of methadone. When he returned our conversation continued.

"What brings you to the methadone program, Jim?"

"I got tired of hustling every day just to get my junk. I'm just sick about holding up mom and pop corner stores. I don't feel right about it. At least I don't have to do that to get my fix of methadone. It keeps me off the street."

Because it was also highly addictive, some felt giving out methadone was simply substituting one drug for another. However, Dr. Fort felt that the methadone did give them a chance to get out of the cycle of crime necessary to support their habit and give them a chance of getting clean. It was all very sad and tragic to me.

Besides Fort Help there were many other interesting tenants in the building: painters, sculptors, musicians etc.

The entire building was being transformed into a mini hippie community. Someone set up a kitchen on the top floor and offered communal meals in the evening for as little as 50 cents. Most, but not all were vegetarian. It was all so new and different to me. They served spaghetti without meat or meat sauce and brown rice and vegetables. And why eat processed breakfast cereal when you could eat granola? Everything was being questioned at that time, including what and how we ate.

What I had long considered a side dish, was now the center of the meal. For example, one night they served baked potatoes and a salad. And by the way, be sure to eat the entire potato, peel and all I was told. That's where a lot of nutrients were, close to the earth.

One of the tenants was offering massage training on the second floor. It was open to anyone in the building and was free. The price was right and what the heck, I was open to just about anything at this time. We chose a partner and the instructor demonstrated the different strokes. Over the course of a couple months, she worked her way through the entire body, starting with the face and head. She called it Swedish / Esalen massage. It was developed at the Esalen Institute in Big Sur along the coast.

Of course we were all naked, so I got concerned as we started working down the body that something might happen that I didn't want to happen. What I discovered was that I loved being touched and touching the opposite sex in a sensual but a non-sexual way. It was really wonderful and soothing. I realized that to be aroused sexually was actually counterproductive to the experience, since it created a tension in the body that wanted to be released. The objective of massage was to go deeper and deeper into a relaxed state. I learned that if you made the commitment to be relaxed and not aroused, it was unlikely to happen.

Meanwhile, back on Fillmore Street there was a little problem with one of the tenants. Tom, the manager of the building told me a Philippino tenant, Juan, on the first floor was having a mental breakdown and that he had started his mattress on fire. Tom was concerned for our safety and worried Juan would burn the building down if something wasn't done. That night Juan knocked on my door and came into my room frantic.

"They're coming after me," he said.

"Who?"

"The police. Please don't tell them I'm here!"

"Are you sure they're coming for you?" I asked.

"Yes, I'm sure. They're coming, they're coming. Close the curtains."

"But why? What did you do?"

At this he runs into my closet, closes the door and won't come out. I didn't know what the hell to do. I was pretty certain that the cops weren't after him and that what he was exhibiting was paranoia up close and personal.

I was in way over my head here. I didn't have any idea

how to handle this. So I called Frank, one of the counselors from Fort Help.

"Frank, I need your help. This guy down the hall is really flipping out. He just ran into my closet and refuses to come out." I explained frantically.

Juan heard me making the call. He bolted out of the closet accusing me of calling the police and telling them where he was. He then dashed out of my apartment and out onto Fillmore Street in his stocking feet. Frank was still on the phone. I'm in a panic.

"What do I do, Frank? He just ran out the door and into the street," I said breathlessly. "Shit, he doesn't even have any shoes on!"

"Sounds like he's having a schizophrenic break. Try to follow him and I'll be right over," he instructed.

Tom joins me and we desperately run down Fillmore trying to find him. I run up to a hooker sitting on a fire hydrant and, breathless, ask her if she's seen him. She looked at me all blurry eyed and slowly said, "Do you want to fuck?" She was obviously no help, so I keep running until I see a cop car driving by slowly.

I run to the passenger side of the patrol car and as the cop slowly rolls down his window, I see that he's drawn his revolver and is pointing it right at me through the passenger door. I quickly explain what's happening. He tells me to go back to my apartment and they'll look for him. I notice he still has his gun pointing at me, so I move away from the car slowly and walk back up the hill where I meet Frank and Tom.

We all drive around for a good half hour but there's no sign of him. The next morning we find out the police found him hiding in an alley and took him in on a seventy-two hour hold. He was then transferred to Napa State (Mental) Hospital. Apparently, what pushed him over the edge was that while he was working on a cat as veterinarian student, he had overdosed the cat with meds and killed it. He feared he would be expelled from school and bring shame on his family. Tom and I visited him a month later in Napa. He was heavily medicated and really out of it. How sad and how fragile the human psyche.

GOODWILL HUNTING

Shortly after this incident, I quit my job at the Children's Art Center and started working for Goodwill Industries. It also qualified as CO work and I was tired of living on the edge. I was now making a whopping $250 per month! I was even able to save a little bit. Best of all I could walk to work.

Granted, it was a long walk, but I didn't mind. I walked down Fillmore, over Geary Ave., the border of the black "ghetto," to California Strett. I passed several vacant lots and blocks lined with black men drinking from brown bags and making drug deals. Sometimes, when I felt a little apprehensive or a little more vulnerable, I'd intentionally cross the street to avoid a large crowd of men.

My job at the Goodwill was to unload and sort the clothes and other donations when they arrived. Occasionally, I manned the cash register. There were many times when there was so little activity that the workers would gather at the back corner of the store and watch TV on a donated television set. Since I was totally uninterested in this, I would bring a book and read during the down times.

Right across the street was a donut shop. They had these great tasting pastries called apple fritters, a totally new treat to me. Near this shop was a Japanese grocery store. I noticed these strange looking patties in the window and learned that they were fried tofu patties. They were only 25 cents each and made a quick and easy dinner full of protein. Apple fritters and tofu patties, who knew this would be the beginning of my new, healthier diet!

The manager of the Goodwill store was an Indian man named Kanar. He didn't seem to like me very much and after a few months he called me into his office and said he was preparing to fire me for reading during business hours. His friend Larry in the Mission St. store had talked him out of it. He offered to have me transferred to his store in lieu of being fired.

I was outraged. Fired. For what! Everyone else was watching TV. I was deeply offended, particularly since I'd never been fired before from any job I'd had. I think the real truth was that unlike the other employees, I was college educated and didn't treat him with enough deference. He liked to throw his weight around and boss people. I wasn't very compliant.

When I arrived at the Mission St., store Larry made it seem like he was doing me a big favor. Though I was grateful that he "saved" me from being fired, I was also resentful. I had done nothing to justify being fired! On the positive side, it was now a safer walk to work.

One of Larry's friend's, Russ, was a regular customer. He dealt in antiques and collectibles and was a tall and handsome guy. He reminded me of a football quarterback. One day he asked me if I would help him carry a dresser to his truck and ride with him after work to unload it. Coincidently he lived in the same apartment building as Larry, so after we unloaded the dresser we walked down to Larry's for a visit before he drove me back to the Mission District.

Larry offered to give me a tour of his apartment. He had a roommate, Marco, and when we got to the bedroom, it slowly began to dawn on me that there was only one bedroom and only one bed in there. Next he showed me his home office. On the wall were several pictures of naked men. Now it's starting to crystallize exactly what was going on here and I'm growing increasingly uncomfortable. My mind was swirling trying to make sense of it all. My heart was pounding but at the same time, I'm trying to look cool.

Russ sat next to me on the couch and Larry and Marco brought in glasses of wine. I debated whether I should get up and run out of there, but knew I was miles from home. Suddenly, Russ puts his arm around me and kind of pulls me closer to him. I pushed him away and yelled, "What the hell are you doing?"

He said, "Relax. You might like it."

I jumped out of my seat and demanded that he drive me back immediately or I'd walk. I was totally freaked out. I climbed into his pickup and we rode silently back to Mission St.. No one ever mentioned the evening again.

It took me a long time to get my head around the idea that a gay person could not only look normal but actually look like a football player. I was also really pissed that Russ had been so aggressive with me and had violated my boundaries so blatantly. I barely said hi to him after this. I also began to view differently my boss Larry's effort to "help me out" by having me transferred to his store.

What an awakening. I didn't have a clue that either of them were gay. Not a clue. I had seen gays on the street but they all seemed to fit the stereotype of the effeminate, girly male. I believe my ignorance in the matter was totally understandable, given that there were no, known to me, openly gay people in Iowa when I was growing up.

On the other hand, there had been rumors floating around the Loras College campus that many of the seminarians living in Rohlman Hall (the seminary dorm) were gay. I even heard the phrase Faggot Hall uttered a few times. It made me laugh. I knew they were full of it. There were no gays living in my dorm!

However, there was the classmate quietly thrown out in the middle of the school year for what was rumored to be inappropriate behavior with other young men. I was skeptical of this at the time. It wasn't until many years later that one of the "cool guys," Paul, whom all the girls were crazy about and another friend Dennis came out as gay, as well as one of my seminary classmates from Des Moines.

It did strike me as strange and bothersome that gay guys were approaching me. There were a few other occasions, not as blatant as with Russ, but just as unnerving. Perhaps it was related to the new identity I'd taken with the move to San Francisco. First of all I was no longer Mike. I made it clear from the beginning that my name was Michael. Mike was tough and macho. Michael was soft and poetic. I preferred the later. I learned that Michael also meant "one close to God." That sounded like a pretty nice position to be in, so from then on I was Michael, except of course whenever I visited Des Moines. There I was still just the same old Mike.

Along with the name change came the conscious change in my attitude toward what it meant to be a man. From the time I was a young boy I strove to prove that I was a man. I learned to swear like the best of them. By observing other men I had perfected just the right harshness and mean facial expression while releasing, "You Mother Fucker!" or "God Damn Son-of-a Bitch!" and of course the mother of homophobic curses, "You Cock Sucker" among others. These could also be combined in a myriad of ways by stringing one or more together. For example, "You-God-Damn-Mother- Fucking-Son-of-a-Bitch!"

Since practically every man smoked in the 50's and 60's, including before and/or after sex, according to the movies, I concluded this must be an important way to demonstrate your manliness. So in 7th grade I started covertly smoking any cigarettes that I could find, including cigarette buds near the curbs and on sidewalks.

Once, Bob Reeves and I had accumulated so many random cigarettes, some filtered, some not that we filled up an entire pack. So as we walked to the Friday night football game at Lincoln High, we started working our way through the pack, one after the other. I remember lighting one and, no matter how hard I drew on it, I got nothing. I relit it and tried again, still nothing. Then I discovered that in the darkness I had pulled out the cigarette and lit the filter end!

Fortunately for my lungs and my general health, I went out for basketball the following year. Since I was determined to be a star athlete, and since for athletes smoking was frowned on, I quit.

Finally, I proved my manhood by repeatedly demonstrating that I could endure serious pain and discomfort without complaint. Above all else, a man never showed any signs of weakness and, even more importantly, no matter how severe the physical or emotional pain, he was never, ever allowed to cry.

As I was growing up, boys were often challenged to prove their "manhood" by exercising their strength and when necessary, their violent nature. The words "pussy" and "mamma's boy" were the ultimate insults and we all worked very hard to avoid these labels, whether by fighting at the slightest insult, playing violent, physical sports like football or later by joining the army. All these things reinforced in our own minds and, just as importantly, in the minds of others that we were real men.

Now I was done with all of that. I would no longer be defined in this way. I was a gentle man, a poet, a non-violent warrior in the pursuit of peace and justice. Slowly I allowed myself to feel the pain and eventually instead of suppressing the tears let them flow outward when I was hurting.

Because I had worked so hard to shed the old notions of manhood and take on this new, gentler, softer identity as a man, it is understandable why some might perceive me as gay. And, since I had been celibate for over four years and had in some ways erased my sexual history and identity, there was a short period where I began to wonder myself. Still I was never attracted to men and soon settled the issue by falling madly in love with every woman who smiled at me.

ARE YOU COMING ON TO ME

Not fully recovered from the shock of Russ trying to seduce me, one night as I made my way down Fillmore St., I saw and heard a party going on in one of the flats. I walked into the crowded living room and soon realized it was filled with women only and they were all dancing with one another. I'd never witnessed anything like it. It was surreal. I tried to ignore the angry stares and decided it would be rude and too obvious if I left immediately, so I stuck around for a couple songs, then got the hell out of there.

I guess I'm a slow learner. Around this same time I

became very interested in a young woman who lived in the neighborhood. We had some friendly conversations and one day I invited myself into her apartment. My horniness must have been showing badly. She looked right at me and said, "Are you coming on to me?"

I had no idea what she was saying. I had never heard the phrase "coming on to me" before and said, "What do you mean?"

She looked at me in disbelief, "You know exactly what I mean, and besides I'm not interested in men."

Then it dawned on me. She's a lesbian. Again, I was clueless. I'd never met a lesbian before and must have assumed they'd have short hair and a masculine demeanor. This woman didn't fit that stereotype at all. She had long blond hair and was very attractive. My whole world was beginning to turn upside down. I crept out of her apartment with my tail between my legs and never saw her again.

It was during this time that the glow of living in San Francisco began to fade and the reality of my situation began to sink in. I became more anxious and unsure and very lonely. Slowly the doubts began to seep into my consciousness. Up to this point I was still committed to continuing my training for the priesthood. Now I was having some serious second thoughts. I felt totally alone, like a tight rope walker without a net and I felt myself slipping into depression. It occurred to me that though as a priest you serve hundreds of people, you are still basically alone. You're with lots of people but you're really with no one closely or intimately.

It looked to me like the life of a priest was a lonely life. Everything inside me was saying no to this kind of life. I need human contact, I need human connection. My current state of isolation and the emotional pain I was experiencing trumped everything else and brought what was really important into a clearer focus. For me it was the prospect of a lonely and isolated life that scared me more than anything. It was a bigger issue for me than the absence of sex at that time.

Not that I didn't consider the lack of sexual activity. I really began to question the value and necessity of celibacy. Is it healthy psychologically to deny the body the pleasure and fulfillment it desires and requires? Not only was direct sexual expression forbidden, but any kind of physical contact. I felt on some level this couldn't be healthy. The whole thing was starting to fall apart for me.

ANOTHER ROBBERY ON FILLMORE STREET

It was rumored that some of the black hustlers in the neighborhood were planning to raid our "white" apartment building and steal anything they could find. Some tenants were putting extra padlocks on their doors, so I did the same. The entire building was anxious and apprehensive.

One day as I was walking to the Sacred Heart School to

do some tutoring, three young black men grabbed me and pulled me in-between two buildings. One of them jammed a small knife or razor into my stomach. "Give us some money," he demanded.

This time around I totally lost my cool and started to plead with them to let me go. I had talked with one of them briefly before and tried to appeal to our common predicament.

"I'm like you," I said, "I don't have any money." It didn't work.

"Then give me some weed." One insisted.

"I don't have any," I said.

"Bullshit," he said. " I know you got some back in your apartment. Take us back there and we'll get it."

"I'm telling you I don't have any money and I don't have any weed. Please let me go," I begged pitifully.

Then, while two of them held my arms, one of the others grabbed my wallet out of my back pocket and took out the only cash that was in there, a $5 bill.

The one guy I casually knew said, "He's all right, man. Let him go." And then walked away, leaving the other two to toy with me.

By this time I had totally given up my power in the situation and was completely at their mercy. When one of the men tried to tear my watch off my wrist, he dropped his razor, let go of my arm and reached down to retrieve it. Seeing my opportunity, I pushed the other one off my arm and ran for my life. By the time I got to the school I was a wreck. My heart was pounding and I was sweating and shaking violently.

One of the nuns saw how disturbed I was and asked what had happened. She was visibly upset and tried to comfort me. It didn't help much, particularly since I knew I'd have to walk back past these guys to get back home that night. They had my number now and there was no reason they wouldn't try the same thing again, if not now then at a later date. I was scared to death.

I was also disappointed in myself. I was unable to call forth the inner strength to fight violence with non-violence. It wasn't working this time. My response was fear and weakness. As a result I was powerless and reduced to begging. My self-esteem took a dive.

When I left the school, I walked three blocks out of my way in order to avoid going past the perpetrators. This second attempted robbery in broad daylight convinced me that it was time to get out of the Fillmore and into a safer place. My world was crashing rapidly.

I began to see the Fillmore for what it really was, a dark and dangerous place, especially for a young idealistic white kid. The gunshots seemed to ring louder and more frequently and a man was stabbed to death right in front of our apartment building. Drug deals were going down all around.

There was a prostitute on my corner and many others.

When a car slowed down as it drove by them, they would ask seductively, "Do you want a date?" It sounded so harmless and fun, like taking a girlfriend to the movies. Unfortunately, I learned just how ugly the whole thing was. Most if not all the girls were addicted to heroin and were controlled by a pimp, who was often nearby or riding in the back seat of a Cadillac with his girl as they cruised the area for customers. If their girl didn't do what she was told, the heroin was withdrawn and/or they were beaten until they complied.

And it gets worse. I learned more from a young neighborhood boy, Jesse, whom I met at the grade school. He shared that his older brother was a pimp. He would methodically "make" girls into prostitutes. The pimp would first lock the young girl in a closet. She would be left there for hours or days until she agreed to turn tricks for him. She had then been "broken." At this point he would get her addicted to heroin and would supply it to her whenever she needed a fix, thus making her totally dependent on him. She was helpless without him and saw him as someone who was helping her out. The pimp, on the other hand had total control of his *ho*.

This type of cruelty was unimaginable to me, and in fact initially I didn't believe Jesse. He must be making this all up to impress me. Sadly, I learned from others, he wasn't.

I had begun living in the Fillmore as kind of a sociological experiment, a way to inform myself of the plight of blacks so I could better help their cause. I had been an outsider looking in at the poverty and despair. But now it was clear I had to get away from this evil environment before I was consumed by it too, the sooner the better. My grand experiment of living in the ghetto was quickly ending. I had to get out of there as fast as possible for my own sanity and my own survival!

Chapter VI

ITS ALL OVER NOW BABY BLUE

I really didn't want to admit it, but I knew that now my "unofficial seminary training in the world" was all over. It's not like I woke up one day and made the decision to quit. It was more like an uncomfortable feeling slowly rising up in my belly. I just knew. I wanted to keep it down, push it down and away. I just couldn't bear the idea of it and the inexorable consequences of it. I didn't want to deal with it, didn't think I'd be able to deal with it. I didn't want it to be true, but it was. I was not going to be a priest. It was over! My training had come to an unceremonious end.

For five years I had been preparing myself to serve as a priest. Everything I did was to further my training and preparation, including the move to San Francisco. I was not prepared for anything else. While I had earlier thought I would join the Marines as a fall back, that was not an option now. I really had no backup plan.

It was much more profound than simply changing careers, say like being a teacher instead of a lawyer, for example. This was a deeper phenomenon, a major life change.

My entire identity had rested on being a priest. To say I was set adrift is an understatement. I remember feeling like my whole life was being turned upside down, like the carpet had been pulled right out from under me. I was totally and completely lost and disoriented.

One of the first things that went through my mind was how was I going to tell my family. I had denied repeatedly that I was doing this to please them, but as soon as I realized I wasn't going to continue, I realized just how much I was doing just that. They would be so disappointed. I had let them down. My mother, my grandmother, my aunts and uncles, everyone who had been so happy that I went in the seminary would now be so disappointed. I couldn't face them, especially my mother.

Making matters worse, I would have to do it face to face. My Uncle Tony died at this time and I flew back to Des Moines for the funeral. During the visit I somewhat off handedly told my mother that I wouldn't be completing my seminarian training, then quickly looked away. I couldn't bear to see her reaction. She didn't say much but I knew she was deeply disappointed. This only fed my sense of shame and embarrassment. I had failed at my mission, unconscious as it was, to please my mother and my family, to make them proud and perhaps to lift their spirits. I didn't realize how important it was to me to make them happy and proud until this moment.

My father's reaction was more muted. Although he had boasted for years about his son the seminarian, it always seemed it was more about how special this made him in the eyes of others rather than the religious blessing that a priest could bring to the family.

In actuality, I think he was always a little ambivalent about it. He was not a devout Catholic by any means, and didn't particularly like being in church. Perhaps it was a reminder of how far he had strayed from the path. The only thing he said to me when I told him I wasn't continuing was that "once you start something you should finish it. Once you decide to do something you should stick to it until the end."

I shot back in a somewhat playful way, "Look who's talking. You've changed your career several times. First you were a carpenter, then you had a manufacturing business and now you're running a bar."

"You got me there. You're right," he responded and smiled.

It was somewhat of a relief that he wasn't all that upset or disappointed. He kind of took it in stride.

Flying back to San Francisco I remember wishing that the plane would crash. That's how despondent I was. I never would have taken my own life, but if the plane crashed, that would be different. I wouldn't be responsible for that. I desperately wanted out! How could I ever put my life back together now. I was completely overwhelmed. Moving forward felt insurmountable. I was in the middle of the most serious crisis of my life and had no idea how to work my way out of it. I knew I couldn't go back home. I had burned that bridge in my mind months ago. I would have to work it out in San Francisco.

In addition to dealing with my family I had to deal with all the friendships and acquaintances that I had formed in San Francisco based on the big lie of who I was and what I was up to. For the sake of having a real life experience, I had been deceitful. I wanted to be seen as and treated as a regular guy and not as a candidate for the priesthood.

It seems ludicrous now, but it was a huge deal then. I felt like a fraud and knew I'd have to muster the courage and go to each person and come clean. I held my situation in the same way a recovering alcoholic apologizes to all those whom he'd hurt along the way.

First I went to Gale from the International Children's Art Center.

"Gale, there's something I need to tell you that's very important. I was not honest with you when I worked here. I wasn't simply a college graduate. I was a seminarian during my college years and was planning to return to the seminary after two years." I confessed.

"Ok," she said.

"Well, I've been feeling really bad about deceiving you and I just wanted to come clean and let you know the truth."

"Hey, it's not a big deal. I'm sorry it's been burdening you."

"Yes, it has been."

"Thanks for letting me know, but really, it's no big deal," she repeated.

To my great relief, as I went to each friend or coworker, they all responded similarly. They weren't upset with me. In fact they seemed very sympathetic to me for having carried the burden. Nonetheless, it was important for me to tell them the truth that I wasn't just a college graduate who had majored in history. I was, or had been in fact, a seminarian.

Then there was Bishop Dingman to deal with. I wrote a very long letter letting him know that I was not continuing. I also let him know how angry I was at the church, along with most institutions. So I wrote a long list of grievances, my own personal 95 Theses:

1. The people were too dependent on the priest for their salvation and as such the priest was actually an impediment to their spiritual growth.

2. Though I would not have chosen it for myself, celibacy should be optional and not mandatory.

3. Women should be allowed to be priests.

4. The church was complicit in the Vietnam War by their silence. They should have condemned the brutality loudly and clearly as immoral, but did not.

5. Women should be allowed to practice birth control and have control over the planning of their families.

6. The priest is unnecessary. We can have our own direct, personal relationship with God.

7. All the doctrines of the church, Sunday obligation, Original Sin, mortal and venial sin etc. were all man made rules and were all a gigantic distraction from the essence of Christ's teachings: To love God, and to love your neighbor as you love yourself. All the other stuff was bullshit.

* For the full text of the original, hand written letter see Appendix, page 169, #2.

JOAN AND JEANNE SAVE MY LIFE

**Jeanne, Michael, Joan In front of their
Delores Street flat**

I met Joan Kiley in front of the U.S. Post Office in Dubuque, Iowa. We had gathered, along with several other students and adults for an hour long "silent vigil for peace" on Sunday mornings. The locals loved driving by and shouting insults at us, but we held firm and took the abuse, Martin Luther King and Gandhi style. We were meeting violence with love, or at least indifference. We were convinced it would help end the madness of the Vietnam War.

Joan showed up with Jeanne McMahon a few months after I landed in San Francisco. They rented an apartment just off Dolores St. and we saw each other occasionally. Fortunately, at the same time I needed to get out of the Fillmore, they decided they needed a larger space.

We all went out apartment hunting and found a lovely second floor flat at 18th and Dolores. I resisted this particular flat initially. It was $220 a month and there was another three bedroom on Guerrero for $150. It was cheap, so I didn't care that it was also a dump. Joan did, and since she had the deposit money, I had to surrender.

My room had a bay window facing out to Dolores St. I threw a mattress on the floor (even bed frames were rejected at the time) and bought a used dresser and chair at Goodwill. I hung an orange blanket on the window for a curtain. I was definitely a hippie now, or at least 80 percent of me was, and I wanted my room to reflect this.

I desperately needed the support and friendship of my roommates as my life was unraveling. And I needed to remove myself from the violence and anxiety of the Fillmore. I credit these two friends for saving my life. I was seriously depressed and in bad shape. Now, I had a family and a nice living environment, a place where I could sort things out.

Shortly after I was transferred to the Mission St. Goodwill, a dark haired, dark complexioned hippie woman walked into the store. She was wearing a dress with jeans underneath and a long, second hand fur coat. She smiled at me and we chatted briefly. I fell in love with her immediately. She said her name was Soham, a middle eastern name, how exotic, and that she lived in Bernal Heights.

After I gave two weeks notice at the store, I prayed she would come in again before I left. On my day off I hung around outside of the store all day so as not to miss her. I was convinced she was the one for me. I even got so desperate that I drove up to Bernal Heights hoping to see her. As I drove up and down the hill, I stopped a few neighbors and asked if they knew her. No luck. Clearly I was a goner.

On my very last day of work I was stunned and overjoyed when she walked into the store. I couldn't believe my eyes. It must be fate! This only reinforced the notion that she was the one, that we were meant to be together. I was determined not to let her go this time before getting her phone number and address. I left the store ecstatic, overjoyed that I had finally found my "soulmate,"

I learned shortly after that she didn't see it quite the same way. She was friendly but somewhat put off and perplexed by my enthusiasm for and infatuation with her. There was also the inconvenient fact that she was already living with someone. However, I didn't let that deter me. I was certain that in time she would discover how wonderful I was and we would have an incredible life together.

This episode with Soham, whom I pursued off and on for some years, demonstrates just how vulnerable and desperate I was. If I could just find the right woman everything would be all right. I just needed to get into a loving relationship. Then I would be able to put my life back together again.

I was a mess and I was looking for someone to rescue me. And not just anyone. It had to be a hippie woman. I didn't want to get pulled back into a typical "middle class" relationship with all the old assumptions and expectations. I wanted an alternative partner to share in my alternative lifestyle, where love and affection were paramount and success and money and material possessions were irrelevant.

In retrospect it was a blessing that Soham and I didn't get together. Because of her repeated rejections and the subsequent pain, I was forced to look inward. I was forced to learn to love myself and feel good about myself rather than rely on someone outside myself to do this for me. This is probably why she and other women shied away from me. They could sense that I was too needy and would be too dependent on them. It was a hard lesson for me to learn and it took me many years, but eventually it sunk in.

* * * *

I didn't stay unemployed for long. I got a job at Mary's Help Hospital in Daly City, just south of San Francisco. I took Larry's place in the business office. He was also a CO and had just completed his two years of service, leaving the position open. He recommended me as his replacement.

Now I was rich. I was earning over $ 400 a month. The only problem was that I hated my job, and my supervisor, Sam, was an asshole. As patients were checking out of the hospital my job was to get them to pay the amount of their bill that their insurance didn't cover. In many cases this was a substantial amount of money.

Some of the patients were still recovering from surgery

or other procedures when they were wheeled to my business office counter. It broke my heart to trouble them with requests, really demands, for money when they were in that weakened state. We weren't supposed to let them leave the hospital until they had paid their bills. If they simply couldn't pay, they would be pressured into signing a promissory note. The hospital knew that once the patient left the hospital it would be more difficult for them to collect.

It felt really heartless to me and as a result I wasn't very good at this collection business. In fact sometimes I let them go without paying or taking only a partial payment or without signing a promissory note. Sam would quickly be all over my case. I was called into his office frequently and reprimanded. The pressure soon became unbearable.

The other thing that was dismaying about working there was the fact that nurses and doctors were constantly smoking in the lobbies and hallways and especially in the cafeteria. They were saying to patients, by their behavior, that smoking was not detrimental to their health. Doctors and nurses surely wouldn't be smoking if it were dangerous or unhealthy. Their actions clearly spoke louder than words. I considered this an outrage.

In fact, most of medical establishment was in denial about smoking in the early seventies. There just wasn't "conclusive proof" that it caused lung cancer or emphysema etc. and ultimately, a painful and premature death.

Amazingly there was even a cigarette dispensing machine just outside the cafeteria. In an act of covert sabotage I made up a label that read, "Cancer Sticks $.50 / Pack" and stuck it over the existing price label. The next day my label was gone, so I put another one up. This cat and mouse game went on for a few more days before I decided to quit before someone smoked out the culprit.

I was also feeling pressure from the radical anti-war environment of San Francisco. In Iowa being a conscientious objector was considered a radical position. In San Francisco it was considered cooperating with the "War Machine." After all, the Selective Service System was merely an unofficial branch of the military. They pulled in the young men and sent them to the Army, who then sent them to Vietnam. What was I doing cooperating with this system? Many of my peers were burning their draft cards, going to prison as draft resistors, fleeing to Canada or whatever else they could do to throw a wrench in the gears of the war machine.

It all had an effect on me. Yes, I realized, it really was just one great big War Making Machine. So after one and one half years of service and with only six months to go, I mailed my draft cards back to my draft board in Iowa and told them I would not be completing the two years of service. I strongly suggested that they should all resign and work to end the war in Vietnam immediately.

I also told them that I was not running and I could be reached at my Dolores Street address. I was prepared to go to prison if it meant helping to stop the war and, almost as importantly, had an impact on others' propensity to violence and war. I fully expected to be arrested and I welcomed it, even though it would likely result in up to two years in prison.

VIVA MEXICO

Now, free from the CO requirement, I gave notice at Mary's Help Hospital, told Sam he was the worst boss I'd ever had, filled my backpack and took off for some R&R in Mexico. I was told by some other travelers that the border guards hated young Americans with long hair and were turning them back at the San Diego and Mexicali borders. So I hitch hiked to Nogales, Arizona and crossed there with my hair carefully stuffed into a cowboy hat.

I stood on a lonely road in Nogales, Mexico for hours trying to hitch a ride but finally gave up. I met a couple of other Americans at the train station, also with long hair. They spoke very good Spanish and started giving me some Mexican travel tips when two Federalies came up to us and escorted one of my new friends, Rich, to a back room. He returned about fifteen minutes later looking rather pale.

"What happened?" I asked.

"Basically they shook me down," he answered.

"What do you mean?" I asked in disbelief.

"One of the Federalies took out his gun and pointed it right at me. He said if I didn't give them some money, they wouldn't let me board the train."

At first I thought he was pulling my leg, but then he went on.

"This is just what they do down here. Bribery is a way of life. They're always pulling this kind of shit," Rich said. "I had to give them twenty bucks. They knew I had no choice."

I guess I shouldn't have been so surprised. I had been told about the bribes that were required to cross the border. His friend and I lowered our heads and prayed they wouldn't take us into the back room also. This idea of having a gun pointed at me wasn't very appealing to me, nor could I afford to give up twenty dollars of my travel fund. Fortunately the train was about to leave, so we all jumped on as fast as we could. We breathed a sigh of relief when we felt the train slowly creeping forward and out of the station.

We traveled all day and into the night until we arrived at Mazatlan. We got rooms in a cheap hotel near the central market and hung out together the next day. The noise level was unbearable. The buses and cars had no mufflers, at least no discernible ones, and it seemed like all the merchants were constantly trying to hustle you as you walked past their stalls. It was not my idea of rest and relaxation.

I learned of a small island just off the coast, Isla de la Pietra. You could practically swim there it was so close, but for eight pesos you could get a ride over on a very small rowboat. Carmela had a makeshift outdoor restaurant near the ferry drop. From there it was about ten miles to the other end where a small village stood. In between were coconut plantations and one long sandy beach.

It was the sandy beach and the quietness I was after, so I hiked about half way down the beach and set up a camp in the sand near the edge of the coconut groves. I made a lean-to out of driftwood and palm leaves and settled in for my own personal week long silent retreat.

It wasn't hard being silent. There was absolutely nobody there. I didn't see anyone until the second or third day when I saw a man and his donkey walking past near the water's edge where the sand is firmer. I laid in the sun, swam in the warm waters and really started to unwind.

I collected some beautiful, large sand dollars, read, meditated and played the guitar I'd bought in Mazatlan. Whenever I got too hot I simply jumped in the ocean to cool off. It was my own personal paradise. At one point I remember speaking out loud and not even recognizing my own voice. How weird. I wondered how much of our identity, and perhaps even our voice, was shaped by our speaking and interacting with others.

About mid-week I was running out of water and was upset that I'd have to hike all the way back to the ferry to get some more. So when the man came by late that day, I waved him over. I spoke very little Spanish and he no English, but we somehow figured out how to communicate with each other. His name was Pablo. He saw the guitar and indicated that he wanted to play it. He sang me a Spanish song, then handed me the guitar and I sang him one in English. This went on, back and forth, for several songs and we were both smiling and enjoying each other's company. At the end, I think he asked if he could have the guitar. I was taken aback and quickly said no. What nerve to even ask.

Before he left, I motioned that I was nearly out of water. He took my canteen and small plastic bottle and said he'd get me some. He lived back in the jungle, he said, and worked at a coconut plantation. When he didn't come back after a couple hours, I began to worry that he had stolen my water containers and I'd never see him again. Then, just before sunset, he reappeared, not only with my water containers but also with a big glass jug filled with water and tied onto a rope, which he had slung over the back of his donkey. I felt like shit for my suspicious thoughts and thanked him profusely.

I was sleeping a few days later when I thought I heard footsteps near me. I assumed it was an animal but didn't want to rise up and look around for fear it might attack me. So I played possum and went back to sleep. The next morning I woke up and looked to my right where I'd laid my backpack. It was gone. The guitar was gone too! I looked down the beach and saw a small orange speck in the distance. It was my backpack.

The thief had thrown all my clothes out on the beach and had taken all my pesos. Apparently he had a bit of a heart. He left a ten peso note in one of the pockets, enough for the ferry so I could get off the island. What he didn't get was the $40 I had put in my pants pocket or the $ 20 dollar bill I had stuffed in one of my boots. I'd seen this in some movie when I was younger. Never put all your money in the same place when you're on the road!

It wasn't over, but I knew I'd have to eventually cut my trip shorter than I had planned. Plus, I was really upset about losing my guitar. It was going to be my travel companion.

My mind went immediately to Pablo. It had to be him. I'd seen no one else. He had also wanted my guitar. My certainty solidified the more I thought about it and my anger rose each time I ran the whole thing through my mind. I threw everything back into my backpack and stomped off into the jungle intent on finding him and retrieving my guitar and money.

I followed a trail that led me to a small dirt floored hut made of palm branches. I asked the woman outside if this was Pablo's house. I assumed she was his wife. She nodded her head, "Si."

"Donde esta Pablo?" I demanded.

"He's working at the coconut plantation," she answered nervously.

"He stole my guitar and money and I'm going into your hut and getting them." I informed her.

"No, no," she said. "He didn't take your money and there's no guitar inside."

I didn't believe her. There was no question in my mind. He had taken both.

"I'm going into your hut to get them," I repeated in broken Spanish, and started for the open doorway. She threw herself in front of the entrance and refused to let me in. I was so angry and outraged that I came very close to pushing her out of the way and forcing my way inside. I hesitated. Still fuming, I stomped back to my campsite.

As I was finishing packing up, I saw a man running toward me yelling. It was Pablo. He swore he hadn't taken anything. He was so sorry I'd been robbed. He offered to give me some food and some money to get off the island. All my certainty about him being the thief evaporated instantly. I was so ashamed that I had accused this good man and was horrified that I had come so close to violating his wife and home.

What a lesson and one that I've carried with me ever since. We can convince ourselves of almost anything, including others ill intentions, building our case bit by bit. But logical conclusions are not necessarily the truth. I had seen no one else all week. He had asked for my guitar. Who else could it have been. It had to have been him. But it wasn't! I knew in that moment it wasn't. I regretted I hadn't just given him the guitar. Now neither of us had it.

I hiked back to Carmela's restaurant where I learned that I wasn't the only one who'd been ripped off. A group of young local men hid in the coconut plantations and swept down on the beach at night and stole from the campers. Some had even lost sleeping bags that they'd spread out during the day to dry.

I took the rowboat "ferry" back to Mazatlán and caught the next bus going south. It was really just an old school bus and it was packed with people, animals and canvas bags filled with anything and everything. The bus stopped frequently wherever people were standing along the highway and groups of locals jumped off as new passengers jumped on.

Both sides of the road were filled with banana plantations as far as you could see and, as the sun began to set, the bananas were transformed into shadowy, exotic plants from another planet. By the time the bus pulled into San Blas, a small sleepy town on the Pacific, I was half asleep. I threw my sleeping bag down on the beach and was lulled to sleep by the undulating roar of the Pacific Ocean.

The next day I bought a roast beef sandwich from a street vendor and later a smoked fish, the entire fish, head and all, from an open pit on the beach. That evening as I camped on the beach all hell broke loose, and I mean all of it. I could not stop it from coming out of both ends of my digestive track. It was the second most miserable night I've ever spent, after nearly freezing to death near Flagstaff.

I was so weak the next day I could barely walk. Everyone that looked at me immediately said an unfamiliar word, "tourista" or "Montezuma's Revenge." All I could think of was the roast beef from the vendor and the smoked fish teaming with flies. It had to be one or the other, or perhaps both.

I wandered listlessly along the beach and by the grace of God ran into Rich from Nogales and Mazatlán. He was so compassionate. He paid for a hotel room and went into town and bought me some Keopectate. I honestly don't know what I would have done without him. I was nearly delirious. He stayed with me for a few days until I was stronger and could take care of myself. What an angel. Then we left together for Mexico City, Guadalajara and finally, Oaxaca.

I loved Oaxaca. It had a whole different combination of European and Caribbean feel to it. I took a bus up the mountain to Monte Alban and walked through the ancient Aztec ruins. It was the highest point in the area and you could see the plains below for miles in all directions. I would have stayed longer, but I was running out of money fast, so I got on a bus to the East and Rich continued on his own.

The road was extremely windy and narrow as it wove through the mountains. It seemed like every bus I rode had a crucifix and /or a statue of Mary on the dash or hanging from the rear view mirror. They gave me little comfort as the bus lurched from side to side. There were no guardrails and the driver, trusting a little too much in the religious icons, repeatedly passed on the sharpest, blindest curves.

Thoughts of my young life ending on a mountainside in Mexico were quickly replaced by numbing nausea followed by uncontrollable vomiting. Though the other passengers were sympathetic, one even offering me a small coin to put under my tongue as a remedy, the driver grew more annoyed with each vomiting incident. At one point he moved me to the front seat overlooking the narrow entrance stairs, thinking that being able to watch the road was the cure. I immediately vomited right onto the stairs.

By the time I landed in the town of Veracruz on the Gulf of Mexico, I was weak and pale and seriously dehydrated. I prayed I'd run into Rich again, but knew I was on my own this time. I had only $10 left to my name. I knew I had to use it wisely if I was going to make it back to San Francisco, but was so depleted I spent $3 on a hotel room instead of camping and then went out looking for something that would settle my stomach and restore my energy.

The night air was so thick I could feel it pressing against my body as I walked. The humidity hung on me like a wet blanket. This was a totally different Mexico. The sounds of tropical birds were everywhere. It looked and felt and sounded like Cuba, and since I'd never been to Cuba, I don't know how I could have to come this conclusion. Perhaps it came from watching Ricky Ricardo on *I Love Lucy*.

I passed a street vendor with a large metal tub filled with what looked like ears of corn, steam rising up through the pile. I was starving but fearful of putting anything irritating in my raw and battered stomach. Maybe a corn on the cob would settle me. As I pulled off the husk I discovered that there was no ear inside but rather a mushy, cornmeal batter filled with cheese. It was my very first tamale! Best of all it was only 25 cents.

When I departed the next morning I was down to $6 or so and had hundreds of miles to go. Though it was nearly impossible to hitchhike in Mexico, I had no choice but to try at this point. Just when I needed it the most, all the grace I'd accumulated in the seminary paid off. I got a ride with an American on his way back to the states. We camped on the beach the first night, and when we hit the U.S. border at Brownsville, Texas the next day, I had $5 in my pocket.

Once over the border I put out my thumb and got a ride to San Antonio where my friend and former traveling companion, Randy, was stationed in the Army. I spent the night with him and his wife, Beth, borrowed $20 and set off the next day hitchhiking back to San Francisco.

SWAMI SATCHIDANANDA SAVED MY LIFE

I'd heard so much about Yosemite National Park that I decided to take a weekend trip to see it for myself. I bought an old wooden backpacking frame from the Goodwill store I had worked at and hooked my Boy Scout pack to it. I'd also kept my promise to myself after nearly freezing to death outside the Grand Canyon, and bought a used down sleeping bag, also from the Goodwill.

I parked on the valley floor and started hiking up the very steep path to Vernal and Nevada Falls. It was very strenuous, so when I saw these two longhaired and bearded hippies climbing effortlessly, I grew curious. Turns out they were devotees of Swami Satchidananda and lived in his San Francisco Ashram not far from me on Dolores Street. They were also brothers, Doug and Tom.

"Why do you guys look like you're out on a leisurely stroll," I asked. "I'm already winded and we're not even half way up."

"We're reciting our mantras while we're climbing," Doug said. "These Mali Beads around our necks help us to keep our minds focused. When we move our fingers to the next bead, we repeat the mantra."

This seemed a lot like saying the rosary to me, and I didn't want to go near those again. At the same time I was very curious.

"If you're interested, you should come by and take some Yoga classes." Doug suggested. "You can either just drop in or sign up for several sessions, which makes each class about $1.50."

This was 1971 and yoga was still very foreign and unfamiliar to most Westerners, including myself. Since I had been thinking about checking out this whole yoga thing, I told them I'd come by and try it out. Plus, since I lived on Dolores Street all I'd have to do is walk a few blocks up the hill, just past Dolores Park.

The spray from the water falls cooled us as we inched our way up the side of the mountain, and the roar of the falls, at times deafening, reminded us of the height of the river above us and the power that was generated from the falling water. At times we had to hold on to a cable to keep us on the steep and narrow path, which was dotted with stone stairs at the steepest points.

When we got to the top, we soon discovered that all the camping spots were taken. So we gathered some pine needles and grass and made ourselves "beds" right on top of a massive boulder. I've slept on some hard beds, but this was ridiculous. It was the third most miserable night of my life.

They took off to the north toward Half Dome and I decided to go the opposite direction and hike along the rim of the canyon by myself. I waded over a couple of rivers and lay in the sun on the other side to dry my legs and feet. The view into the canyon was beyond description. We didn't have anything like this in Iowa! It turned out to be the most beautiful hike I'd ever taken. Just breathtaking. From that day on I was hooked on backpacking and getting away from the maddening crowd and into the serenity of the natural world.

I was definitely warm enough this time in my down bag. However, I suffered badly from the make shift equipment. The backpacking frame dug deeper into my back with each step and, speaking of my back, the grass and pine needle beds were sorely inadequate. The mosquitoes also had a heyday. I resolved right then to invest in some decent equipment and some super strong mosquito repellent.

I drove my little red Anglia back to San Francisco on Monday. Though the Yosemite trip was wonderful, the glow didn't last long. I was still left with what seemed like an insurmountable problem - namely, how to put life back together again after leaving the seminary. I was anxious and despondent and wasn't sleeping well. In a word, I was a wreck.

Later in the week I hiked the three blocks up to 21st and Dolores to this magnificent three story Victorian mansion. There was a beautiful wooden sign in the center of some sort of mandala. It read The Integral Yoga Institute. As soon as

I entered I could feel the spiritual vibration and smell the incense. I could also feel the good vibrations coming from the hippie men and women, all spiritual seekers, who filled the house. These were my kind of people.

I climbed the stairs to the top floor attic. It had been converted into a yoga room with a beautiful circular tower in the corner. The room was packed with students. We started with some Sanskrit chanting. I had no idea what was being said and I felt resistant to mouthing something I didn't understand. They had finally changed the Latin Mass to English and I wasn't about to go backward. There was also a picture of Swami Satchidananda and another guy on the alter in the front of the room. The teacher bowed to the alter very reverently. I was beginning to have some real doubts about this whole scene.

At the same time I was adventurous enough and maybe desperate enough to try anything that might help reduce my anxiety and stress. I tried very hard, probably too hard, to get into every asana (posture). Some were not that difficult for me. Others were. We were told not to strain. To come out of the asana gently if we felt uncomfortable. I wasn't listening. I didn't want to stand out and look like a beginner, which of course, I was, so I stayed in the pose no matter how uncomfortable I was.

At the end we were led into a "deep relaxation" (Yoga Nidra) process, first tightening, then dropping each limb, the buttocks, the shoulders etc. Then we went through each body part with our minds, breathing gently to release any tension we discovered. Next, we were told to observe our thoughts as they passed through our minds, to think of them as clouds passing by. Finally, we observed our breath, in and out, in and out.

By the time we got to the end I was in the deepest state of relaxation I'd ever been in. And all this without Valium! I never knew it was possible. I was hooked. The best part was that I could create this state on my own at any time. You don't need to be in class. You can do yoga in your room or nearly anywhere you want. I've even been known to do it at the airport while waiting for a flight, much to my daughter's embarrassment.

This was all followed by some pranayama (breathing exercises) and a brief meditation. The whole routine, the asanas, deep relaxation and pranayama became invaluable tools that I've used many, many times since. There have been numerous occasions when I've felt disturbed or out of balance and have gone into a quiet room and done my yoga routine. It takes about an hour if I do the entire series, but usually at the end I feel so much better, mentally and physically. I feel calmer and clearer.

I've often thought what would have become of me if I hadn't discovered Integral Yoga and these simple, ancient survival tools. Of course one never knows for sure, but the emotional pain was so severe it's quite possible I would have turned to drugs and/or alcohol for relief. What a blessing to meet the two yogi backpackers and be led to such a beautiful and powerful teacher and teachings, and all within walking distance of my flat!

The yoga classes brought me into contact with Swami Satchidananda himself. He would visit the Dolores Street

Ashram occasionally and would also give public talks in the San Francisco Bay area. I learned that he was an enlightened master and had been one of the first Indian gurus to come to the west. He had also opened the Woodstock Festival in New York in 1969 by leading a chant of OM (the sound/name of God). There were thousands of devotees all over the world and when he spoke, we all listened intently, wanting the answers to life's mysteries and meaning.

One of the things I loved from the start was Swami's approach to other religions. Instead of putting them down or invalidating them, he acknowledged them and welcomed them, organizing and participating in many ecumenical services over the years with Rabbis, priests, ministers, monks etc.

He once said that there are many paths up to the top of the mountain. You take yours and I'll take mine. You don't need to force everyone to take your path. It doesn't really matter which path you take. They all lead to the same place anyway, they all lead to the top of the mountain, they all lead to God. Swami was well known as an ambassador of toleration and ecumenism and this spirit is captured in his signature phrase: The Truth is one, The Paths are Many.

Within a year of my first yoga class I was off to Lake County to attend my first silent yoga retreat. After this first one, annual New Year's retreats were held at La Casa de Maria outside Santa Barbara, overlooking the Pacific. Ironically, for many years prior it had been a Catholic retreat center. A large crucifix remained at the front of the chapel.

As I attended retreat after retreat over the years, the juxtaposition of Swami Satchidananda sitting cross-legged under this huge crucifix struck me as symbolic of my own personal spiritual journey, starting with the teachings of Jesus and evolving and blending with the teachings and practices of the East. They both live in me now, and I in them.

The first retreat was by far the most difficult. Swami talked about the "self" versus the "Self" and other eastern religious ideas: That God lives within each of us, that we don't have to go searching for peace outside ourselves. It lives within each of us. The ego or mind doesn't want us to remember who we truly are. It wants to be in control. I tried very hard to understand these concepts from a Western perspective. I just couldn't make any sense of it initially.

In response to a retreatant's question: "Who am I really?" Swami said the following:

"Unless we realize our own true nature, unless we become aware of our spiritual reality, our life's purpose is not fulfilled. The main goal behind all these searches and approaches and actions is to realize our true nature, to realize the Self, the God within, and thus to realize that everything is the expression of that same Spirit. Until and unless that happens in our life, we will have to be born again and again. We will have to die many times. That is the one and only goal behind our existence.

It doesn't matter what you do, your goal should be to come close to this understanding: 'Essentially I am God's spirit, I am the pure Self. I am Existence-Knowledge-Bliss Absolute.' Ascertain your true nature, your spiritual nature. You are only functioning through this body and mind. They are your vehicles. You are not the body. You are not the mind. But you are that immortal soul."

Then there was the chanting and the bowing and adoration that were directed to Swami. I was put off by it. I'm not about to surrender to any authority, not after my experience with the Catholic Church and the U.S. Government. And, as I said, I really want to know what I'm chanting rather than blindly repeating what I'm told. The Latin mass was bad enough. I wasn't going down that road again.

Ah, but the silence. That was different. Being in a retreat with lots of people but not talking or interacting with them was very special and powerful. You are forced to look inward and not outward. At first there was a fear of what I might find. Maybe I wouldn't like what I saw. Maybe I'm really screwed up in ways in which I'm not even aware. But after the first day or so, I began to sink deeper and deeper into a blissful space. And how precious it is in our busy lives to have a time where you don't have to interact with others, where you can be quiet and explore your inner life and get closer to the spirit within.

All the meals served at the retreats and his ashrams were vegetarian. Though he never required it of his followers when they were on their own, he did encourage us to consider it. "If you want to grow in your spiritual practice you should be loving to all living beings, even the animals," he would say. "You should refrain from harming any living thing."

I took this to heart. It also fit in with my desire and frustration to end the Vietnam war and all the killing going on there. If I couldn't stop the actual war, I could at least reduce the level of killing and violence in my own life. I felt deeply it was the right thing to do.

However, I was really enjoying sharing dinners with my roommates Jeanne and Joan and I didn't want to disrupt this or have the hassle of needing to prepare two separate meals, one vegetarian, one not. So I put off making the switch for nearly a year until I finally decided I just had to do it. It was in fact an inconvenience, but it was manageable. That was in 1973 and I haven't eaten any meat, chicken or fish since.

A major part of the counter culture revolution at the time was a rejection of materialism and a turning to the spiritual. If the United States was the epitome of materialism, then India was the epitome of spiritualism. We turned to India and the gurus or teachers for the answers and looked to them to lead us in a more meaningful, spiritual direction. Swami Satchidananda was one of those teachers and he had a profound effect on me and many other seekers

He had such a peaceful presence that you couldn't help but be affected. He once said that the most important thing to him is his peace of mind. Nothing is more important. And what spoke to me personally was his comment that before you can bring peace to the world, you must first become peaceful yourself. Before you jump in the lake to save a drowning person, you better first learn how to swim. Otherwise there will be two drowning people. This comment set me on a new mission: To work on myself. To become that peace that I desired so that I could be an effective instrument for peace in the world.

Swami also spoke to our desire for happiness. He reinforced what we all felt at the time, namely, that material things, power or prestige would never bring us lasting happiness. We knew deep down that looking for things or for other people to make us happy was not going to work in the long run. We wanted something more, something more meaningful and enduring. He pointed us inward, he directed us to look within to that spiritual place inside each of us where happiness and peace reside.

And you didn't have to accept this on faith. You didn't have to believe it because some authority says so, you can experience it for yourself through meditation, various forms of yoga, etc. We were ripe for this approach. We had been misled too often by the church and by the government, both of which demanded unquestioning, blind faith. We'd had enough blind faith. That's what got us into Vietnam. We couldn't trust that. But our experience, that we could understand and, over time, learn to trust.

This approach to spirituality was very appealing to me and helped me make the transition from Catholicism and the priesthood to eastern religious thought and practices. I was now on my way to putting my life back together again. A new and, hopefully improved me was taking shape. It wouldn't be easy and it wouldn't be quick. I knew this. But I was on my way. At least, I was on my way.

Epilogue

As I became more deeply engaged in life and took on the responsibilities of a husband, a father and a business owner, I often fell back on these early teachings and practices to help me get through, to help me stay centered and peaceful. I didn't take many formal yoga classes but did develop my own practice at home, where I did yoga and meditated nearly every day.

And at the end of each year I always made sure to take time to attend the silent New Year's retreats where I could renew and refresh myself in the beautiful silence. By the end of seven days of yoga, meditation and just relaxing, I always felt reconnected to the peace within. I was ready to face the world again.

In the evenings after dinner Swami would give a spiritual talk and then answer questions. No, we didn't verbally ask the questions. The silence was maintained until the very end. We would write them on index cards and pray he would get to ours before the end of the evening. We were all searching for answers, so now was our big chance to hear them from an enlightened master from the East. I'm talking about the big, universal questions like: What is the purpose or meaning of life? Who are we and what are we doing here? What happens after we die? And, of course, why are we all here instead of at a New Year's Eve party?*

---

*A sample of the many responses Swami gave to students' questions can be found in the Appendix. on page 188, # 8

After escaping the confines of the Catholic Church, which demanded unquestioning obedience and submission to its rules and doctrines, I was very hesitant to submit to a guru or teacher. As a result, while others bowed reverently to Swami and seemed to be completely enthralled by him, I resisted. I took what I could from the practices and talks and books, but kept my distance from the guru. I wasn't about to surrender my will to another. I wouldn't allow myself to fall under anyone's spell.

Many considered themselves devotees of Swami and even went so far as to be "initiated" into the path. They were given spiritual names, like Rama or Krishna, etc. I did not. I hung around the edges, took in what seemed valuable to me and let the rest go.

Of course there are spiritual writings that suggest that surrendering one's ego is a necessary step for one's spiritual deepening and growth. This would be equivalent to the Christian teaching of — "not my will but thy will be done." This notion would occasionally surface in the back of my mind but was quickly ignored.

But then one day on a yoga retreat several years later it happened. I guess we all evolve or perhaps it was in a moment of weakness or humility. I walked up to Swami during one of the evening programs and with tears in my eyes, got down on my knees and — bowed to him. I told him that I'd been holding back, resisting. I didn't want to call him my guru but in actuality, he was, and had been for some time. I asked for his blessing. He looked at me with understanding eyes, placed his hands on my head and blessed me. I walked back to my seat on the chapel floor.

I'd like to say that bright lights went off and I ascended into a state of perpetual bliss, but it wasn't like that. The lighting in the chapel remained the same and I remained on my seat, eyes still watery. At the same time it was a profound moment for me; an acknowledgment that I couldn't do it alone. I couldn't do it by my own powers. I needed help and guidance. It was also an acknowledgment of what I'd already received from him over the years. It was an expression of my gratitude.

The reluctance I had in surrendering to the guru had also extended to God himself or herself. I refused to use the term, preferring instead "the universe" or "the higher power" or even "the cosmic consciousness." I just couldn't bring myself to speak the word. It seemed so silly and childlike to think there was a God-like fatherly figure up in the clouds of heaven looking down on us.

I was focused on the second half of the two great commandments, "love your neighbor as you love yourself," and had pretty much abandoned the first, "love the lord your God with your whole heart . . ." Since man is made in the image and likeness of God, I reasoned, then by loving my neighbor I was in fact loving God. This allowed me to avoid the issue of God head on.

Perhaps in this case, over time, I had outgrown my battle with the Catholic Church and the need to distance myself from all the guilt and shame it produced in me. I slowly became more comfortable with the name and concept of God. That there was a higher power guiding and directing me, of this I was certain. I'd had too many experiences that validated this. So what difference does it make what name I assign to this power?

I've come to see it as a benevolent power and not one out to punish me. I realize now that God is on my side and wants what's best for me and my loved ones. That doesn't mean that we always get what we want. I've learned that what I want is not necessarily what's best for me. Swami would say, "Man proposes and God disposes." In other words, if it's right for you to have it, God will allow you to have it. If it will not serve your higher good, then you will not have it, no matter how much effort you put into getting it.

Unfortunately, after several years of New Year's Retreats in Southern California, Swami Satchidananda decided to build a Lotus Temple on the East Coast. At that point all the energy and attention shifted from the West to the East coast. Eventually, the annual New Year's Retreats on the West coast ended.

Surprisingly, a couple years ago, after a 25 year absence, The Integral Yoga Institute decided to put on a New Year's retreat. I was thrilled to learn it would be held at the same place, Casa De Maria.

My wife, Shirley, and I attended. We shared a room together but, because we both honor and cherish the silence, we did not speak to each other the entire retreat. Being there brought back a lot of memories. I remembered Swami's evening talks in the chapel and the magic of being with a hundred people in silence The following poems were written during this last retreat.

SWAMI'S IN THE CHAPEL

Swami's in the chapel, so peaceful, so beautiful.
I'm quiet inside too,
in his presence.
Then he tells a joke, a play on words.
I'm lighter. Is this enlightenment?
It must be. I feel so,
light hearted.
No need to take all this spiritual stuff,
nor myself, too seriously.

I want some more of this. That's why I'm here.
To go deeper,
and come out the other end,
laughing.

WHAT'S LEFT UNWRITTEN

I was found, then I was lost,
I was in, then I was out.

When I was in the seminary, studying to be a priest,
I had attained a certain level of peace.

Then I came to San Francisco,
And it all went to shit.

But I walked up Dolores Street
And started doing Yoga and chanting Sanskrit.

I found a guru, but wasn't looking for another Pope,
I'd been down that road before,
No thanks, I'm no dope.

Bow to him all you want,
But that's not for me.
I'll hang around the outside
And wait and see.

I fought it with all my might,
But desperately wanted some peace,
So one day I bowed too, surrendering,
Whole yet incomplete.

APPENDIX

1. Seminary Schedule & Program, St.Pius X Seminary (Rohlman Hall)

DAILY SCHEDULE FOR PIUS X SEMINARY

Monday through Friday:

6:50	Mass Morning prayers in private Breakfast
8:00 - 12:00	Class / Study Atmosphere above first floor
1:00 - 4:00	Class / Study Atmosphere above first floor
4:30	Mass (except Wednesday when the seminarian will participate in Mass elsewhere on campus).
7:00 - 9:30	Study Atmosphere above first floor
10:00	Room check
10:15	Chapel, followed by period of quiet

Saturdays:

6:50	Mass, morning prayers, breakfast
9:00 - 10:00	Room cleaning
10:00 - 12:00	Study Atmosphere above first floor
11:00	Mass
10:00	Late recreation below first floor until

midnight. Each student will sign in at the information office by 10:00 P.M. unless he has chosen Saturday night for his night out. Night prayers in private on Saturday.

Sunday:

9:00 AM	Mass in Christ the King Chapel
7:00 AM	Spiritual Conference
7:30 - 9:30 PM	Study Atmosphere above first floor
10:00 PM	Room check followed by period of quiet night prayers in private.

ROLHMAN HALL PROGRAM   1968-1969

In its decree on priestly formation, the Second Vatican Council directed that: "The rules of discipline should be applied in accord with the age of the students so that they can gradually learn to govern themselves, to make wise use of their freedom, to act on their own initiative and energetically, can know how to work along with their confreres and lay people as well." (IV, II) In conformity with this ideal, the rules of St. Pius X Seminary have been gradually modified in recent years to help the students develop a sense of personal and community responsibility, for freedom demands responsibility.

Responsible freedom, the demands of community living, and obedience to an "authority of service" necessitate priestly discipline. "The discipline required by seminary life should not be regarded merely as a strong support of community life and charity, for it is a necessary part of the whole training program designed to provide self-mastery, to foster solid maturity of personality, and to develop other traits of character which are extremely serviceable for the ordered and productive activity of the Church." (IV, II). It is in fulfillment of these directives of the Vatican Council that the following guides are established:

A. SPRIITUAL DEVELOPMENT

1. The Eucharistic Liturgy must be the sign and source of unity in Christ for our community of seminarians. The seminarians, therefore, will meaningfully participate in the Mass celebrated each day in the Rohlman Hall chapel and the 9:00 Mass on Sundays in Christ the King Chapel. On Wednesdays each week, they are encouraged to participate in Mass with the lay students in the other campus chapels. This will deepen their realization that they are part of the larger Loras community.

2. Each seminarian will make his meditation during any of the following times each day: before or after Mass, before or after night prayers, or at another time approved by his spiritual director.

3. Without exception he will attend the weekly spiritual conference on Sunday night at 7:00. (If worthwhile educational or cultural events occur at the same time, the conference could be rescheduled. The decision will be made by the Rector. Requests for a change of time for the Sunday night conference must be presented to the Rector, Vice-Rector, or Spiritual Director by the preceding Friday night at 10:00.)

B. COMMUNITY LIVING AND PERSONAL
   DEVELOPMENT necessitates the following:

1. The seminarians will observe the following study hours:

> Monday through Friday, 8:00 A.M. 12 noon;
> 1:00 - 4:00 and 7:00 - 9:30.
> Saturday morning, 10:00 - 12:00 noon.
> Sunday evening, 7:30 - 9:30.

During these times a "study atmosphere" is to be maintained above the first floor. This will be achieved only if the seminarians do not unnecessarily visit rooms, carry on loud and unnecessary conversations, or play radios or record players. Since our IDEAL is the Christian community, founded on personal responsibility, we do not have a merit / demerit system or enforcement / punishment system for violations of the study atmosphere. A reminder by the men who have been disturbed will often suffice to correct such thoughtlessness. But since we are all reticent in "correcting" our neighbors, it is suggested that anyone who is disturbed during study hours contact a counselor who will talk to the persons involved.

2. The television set may be used: a. during recreation periods. b. during the evening study periods. Freshmen are encouraged not to spend too much time on TV until they are fully aware of the demands of college academic life and study habits have been well established.

3. The recreation room is not to be used during the morning and afternoon study periods for other than study / discussion purposes.

4. Musical instruments are not to be played in student rooms during study periods. During recreation periods, an individual seminarian may practice softly in his room with the door closed. Group "jam sessions" should always be   held in the basement. The electric guitars are never to be played in student rooms. They can be played in the center garage or in the ironing room only.

5. Pizza may be ordered, but it must be delivered before night prayers. (c.f. Loras Student Handbook p. 31). Popcorn is to be popped in the basement, but not after night prayers. The table and floor must be cleaned after the popcorn is prepared.

6. The inter-communication system is to be used only to call students to the information office, and should not be used for personal conversations.

7. Consideration for others extends into times other than study hours. Therefore, during recreation periods, radios and record players are to be played at low volume so as not to annoy others. The doors to the rooms should be kept closed when playing radios, record players, and musical instruments.

8. Smoking is permitted in the student rooms, recreation room

and the lounges, but not in the corridors, reading room or stairways.

9. Seminarians may receive off-campus visitors in the parlors provided for that purpose. The parlors are not to be used as study places. There is sufficient room in the lounges for that.

10. Typing is not to be done in student rooms after 11:00 P.M. If necessary, one may do his typing in the rooms on the first floor after 11:00.

11. Proper dress for Sunday Mass and spiritual conferences is suit or sweater and tie.

12. The time after chapel at night is to be a period of quiet. This will give each student the opportunity to read, reflect, pray, study, or to retire early without distraction or interruption. Ample time is available for visiting earlier in the day. If a student feels that it is necessary to enter into discussion with others after chapel, he should come downstairs to the lounges to do so. This is not to be a time of recreation except on Friday and Saturday nights.

13. Students in Rohlman Hall are not to have cars without the special permission from the Rector. Those who receive such permission from the Rector are subject to the automobile regulations contained in the Loras College Student Handbook, pp. 24-29. Special attention is called to the fact that they are to use the student parking lots —not the area around Rohlman hall.

14. Spare rooms in Rohlman Hall are to be kept vacant at all times. They are not to be used by students for storing luggage or for study. The furniture is not to be moved from these rooms because they will be frequently used for guests.

C. CAMPUS ACTIVITIES AND OFF CAMPUS PERMISSONS:

The student of Rohlman Hall is responsible for the image of Pius X Seminary and for bearing witness to its purpose and ideals. He must be aware of this responsibility in his activities away from the building.

1. Each student may select two "free week-ends" during the first quarter and two during the third quarter of the school year. He is to obtain a week-end card from his floor counselor and return it to the Rector's office prior to his departure. In choosing these week-ends, he should use foresight in considering coming family celebrations, weddings, etc.

2. Friday night will be the normal night out each week. (Saturday night may be substituted for a good reason.)

Freshman will return to the hall and sign-in by 11:30 p.m. on Friday.
Sophomores and juniors will sign-in by 12:00 p.m.
Seniors will sign-in by 12:30 a.m.

On Saturday evenings students will sign-in by 10:00 p.m. (unless they have chosen Saturday for their free night.) A counselor will be on duty in the information office on Friday and Saturday nights. Each student is to sign-in personally on these two nights.

3. In accord with the practice in the other dorms on campus there will be a room-check by the counselors at 10:00 p.m., Sunday through Thursday. Each student is to be in his own room at that time in order to facilitate this check. If a student is away from the building at the time of the room-check, for some approved activity, he is to sign-in at the information desk upon his return to the building.

4. The general policy regarding the sign-in sheet in the information office:

> a. All students will sign-in on Fridays and Saturday nights.
>
> b. A student who is away from the building at 10:00 room check for an approved activity will sign his name, the time of his return, and the reason for his absence. Approval for events that will keep a student away during room-check must be obtained in advance from the Rector or Vice-Rector.

D. PROBATION AND SEVERANCE FROM THE COMMUNITY:

Those failing to live up to the ideals and rules of Pius X Seminary will ordinarily be helped and corrected by their counselors and brother seminarians. However, at times, violations may be so frequent or of such a serious nature as to raise question about the advisability of keeping a certain member in the community. The penalty of probation will be invoked in such cases to serve as a warning to the seminarian.

1. Each of these cases will be considered individually by the Seminary administration.

2. Major offenses would ordinarily include:

> a. absence from the Hall after room-check or beyond the sign-in time on occasions when late permission has not been granted.
>
> b. violation of the rules regarding alcoholic beverages. Special attention is called to the Loras College rules regarding the use and possession of intoxicants (c.f. Student Handbook, pp. 22-24). These regulations will be strictly adhered to by all residents of Rohlman Hall.

3. When it becomes necessary to place any seminarian on probation, his Diocesan Vocation Director will be notified.

4. Lifting the penalty of probation or suspensions will be determined by the Seminary Administration.

E. ROOM CARE

1. Each seminarian is responsible for keeping his room clean and in good order. His bed should be made each morning before going to class. He is to give his room a general cleaning each Saturday morning from 9:00 to 10:00 a.m.
2. Clean sheets will be issued each Friday. The used sheets should be placed outside each door on Monday morning.

3. There are to be no signs or pictures attached to the outside of student's doors, nor are nails to be used to attach articles to walls of the rooms. Lists of books for sale may be posted on the door at the beginning of each semester.

F. COUNSELORS:

Two seniors have been elected as counselors for each floor. They occupy the following rooms: 216, 240, 316, 340, 416, 440. It is their task to be of special help to the new seminarians and to serve their floor's residents in all aspects of the seminary living.

2. My letter to Bishop Dingman upon withdrawing from the seminary, 1972

Fall '72

Michael A. Gillotti
451 Dolores St.
San Francisco, Calif.
94110

Bishop Maurice Dingman
Diocese of Des Moines
Des Moines, Iowa

Dear Bishop Diagman,

How are things in Des Moines? I'm still in San Francisco, where everything is relatively well, considering the recent elections and the fact that the Vietnam war mutilates onward.

I'm writing you now to inform you that I will not be returning to the Des Moines Diocese to continue training for the ordained priesthood. When I spoke to you over two years ago I was determined to go to San Francisco, complete my two years of alternative service as a conscientious objector, and then return to the diocese to be further trained and ordained. I think you deserve to know why I've changed my mind, and I welcome the opportunity to explain myself.

I'm going to be very blunt, but I hope you won't interpret my frankness as vindictiveness. I simply don't want to chance misunderstanding by dressing my thoughts in euphemisms.

While there is much which influenced my decision, I'll concentrate on the two major reasons or bases for my departure. The first is an inability to associate with an organization whose official positions are contrary to reason and, in some cases, the teachings of Christ himself. The second is a personal evolution of theological thought and the inability of a priest to implement that thought. Ultimately I must be true to my own personal beliefs and while I don't feel they are incompatible with true Christian beliefs, they are incompatible with the traditional Catholic expression of Christian beliefs.

I.) To start with the first reason, then, I feel that the Church has either taken a strong position on issues that are unimportant, or a weak or no position on matters of grave consequence, such as the Vietnam War. The overall image of the Church (or what the Church represents to the world) presented by the accumulation of official positions leaves me unable in conscience to be associated with the Roman Catholic Church, not only as a priest, but even as a layman. (Of course I'll always be a member of Christ's true Church — the church of lovers; and I'll always be a priest, bringing the word of God, or love, to the people of God; but the discrepancy is far too wide between the church Christ spoke of and what we now think of when we say Catholic Church.) I'm afraid that the church has become in the minds of most people in the world an anachronism which few take seriously any more.

Six specific issues come to mind immediately. I'm sure there are more, but for the sake of exemplification and brevity, I'll delineate these six only.

1.) The first, and probably the most single absurd, is the official position of the Church on artificial birth control. Absurd because the majority of Catholics are using artificial devices and many priests are quiet despite the prohibition. Absurd because one man can sit in Rome and dictate to all of Cathodom what is a moral sex life.

2.) The second is celibacy. This is almost as rediculous as the first, since a man's marital status has nothing to do with being a priest - or spreading the word of God. Surprising as this might seem to you, this issue did not of itself influence my decision, since I would have opted for celibacy had I been ordained. The point is, each man should have a choice. I am convinced there is no intrinsic relationship between celibacy and the priesthood.

3.) The third is the ordination of women. And I thought society was finally beginning to recognize women as equally members of the human race. I know if I were a woman I would burn my Church membership card after this insult.

4.) The fourth is a local issue, building a new Dowling High School. I am strongly opposed to the enormous expense of money and energy considering the product — most commonly either obsequious company men or atheists. It also tends to isolate Catholics and divides us from our brothers in a society already inundated with divisiveness.

5+6.) The fifth and sixth are interrelated and are also the most sensitive, the first being abortion and the second the Vietnam war and all war. First of all, I have been unable to resolve the question of abortion in my own mind. But whether I would or would not have an abortion is really not the issue. The issue is whether morality should be legislated. To this I am adamantly opposed, especially since laws against moral activities seldom prevent the activities, they merely push the action further underground. This is a decision each woman must make, and no one, especially males, have the right to make that decision for her.

The issue takes on an added dimension when you consider that thousands of dollars and

hundreds of hours of energy was spent by
Catholics officially and unofficially to prevent
liberalized abortion laws in Iowa and other states,
while only a trinkle of money and energy has been
expended to bring the war in Vietnam and all
wars to an end. How many of the anti-abortion
picketers have done anything to bring the war to
an end? I'd be surprised if it were very many.
And how many issues of the Catholic mirror or
other Catholic newspapers have strongly or even
mildly condemned our governments policy in Endochina?
I've been reading the mirror every week for over
two years, and have found nothing but the smallest
articles about the war or war in general. The
headlines of every paper should burn with rejections
of the war because we are Christians. Yes, every
issue, til every Catholic is sick of it, til every
Catholic knows that to be a Christian and a
Catholic and be part of any war is a contradiction
that no one can escape, no one can turn his
head to.

And you bishop, how many statements have
you made? I've been listening, but hear none.
How many times have you pleaded with your flock
to put aside the attitudes of war and violence and
revenge and to adopt the spirit of love and concern
as Christ taught? How many times? And how
many bodies are left burned and mutilated in
Southeast Asian villages as the pages of the mirror
talked of Dowling, or can non-Catholics receive
communion or how evil abortion is, or the altar of
St. Peters. I want to scream, I want to cry,
I want to run up and yell in your ear until
even one strong word against the war drops out.
I am outraged by your silence.

II. The second major reason involved in my decision not to be formally ordained is an evolution in theological thought — a different view of God and salvation than what the Church is passing out and set up to pass out.

I believe that most of the activities of the Church and the functions of the priest are completely superfluous to deepening a relationship with God and to salvation or personal happiness. In fact, the Church as it is today may impede a person's finding happiness by diverting his attention. People need not go through all the liturgies, ceremonies, meetings, they don't even need to go through Catholic schools to find the peace of Christ. All we need do is following Christ's example and his two great commandments in all that we do, love God and love each other.

Unfortunately, this message of salvation and happiness is obscured in the barrage of activities priests present to the people. Most people, then, develope a dependency on the priest. They rely on the priest to save them — to think for them, to interpret scripture for them, to make moral decisions for them, to bring them in touch with God — so that when the priest is removed, so is their entire spiritual life. This is like a child who must be fed by its parents. I say no, just as a child learns to feed himself, so must we learn to feed ourselves spiritually. But as long as the parish remains structured the way it is, where large groups of people go through a sterile ceremony once a week and change out of their Sunday clothes as soon as they return home, most Catholics will be content with being spoon fed and never grow to mature and responsible Christians. It's much easier the way it is. Who is really moved to be responsible for themselves when someone else consistently assumes responsibility for them.

If you doubt what I say, discontinue masses on Sunday and see how many people cry for their ritual. If there has been a spirituality established within each individual, then while the liturgy may be nice and beneficial, it will not be essential to that person's spiritual life.

The spirit is within each of us. To grow close to that spirit, to grow close to God is the goal of the Christian. And having grown close to the spirit within, we will immediately be united to his brothers, who bear the same spirit. And of course we'll love each other, then, as Christ loved us, because we are of the same spiritual body; and just as you would not tear off an arm and stomp on it, you would not harm another member of your spiritual body — if you knew he were a member.

That's all there is to Christianity, and that's all there should be to Catholicity, if it is to be truly an expression of Christianity. It's that simple. Christ even said this explicitly in the two great commandments:

"You shall love the lord your God with all your heart, and with all your soul, and with all your mind. . . . . 'And . . . you should love your neighbor as yourself (matt. 22:37)"

And now you tell me how that simple message is retained and reflected in the structures and organizations of the Catholic Church. I honestly can't find it. And the mass, the institution which Catholics are in most contact, does not state this principle clearly. The mass is an impersonal and boring experience for most people, they just don't want to admit it, because there's no alternative. It's either the mass, or no practice of their religion.

So how can we expect Catholics to encorporate this principle of love of God and man into their lives when they are not provided with adequate tools, with tools that really bring them peace. I personally feel that if people were shown how to meditate on the peace within in and were encouraged to do this regularly, everything else would fall in place. Liturgies and other activities would flow from this into really meaningful events.

But instead liturgies are composed and imposed on people by liturgical counsels far removed from their daily lives. And peoples' minds are cluttered with meetings, birth control, confession, sins, supporting catholic schools, divorce laws, marriage laws, burying laws, communion laws, ordination laws, boring sermons which often have nothing to do with surviving in contemporary society, and ironically the biggest obstacles of all to this simple message of love, the priests, bishops and the pope himself a sinile old man who really does think he's God or has a special contact with him that no one else has. When actually every person has the spirit within him, has God within him, and all we need do is become aware of his presence. Is it not written that we are made "in the image and likeness of God." But instead of trying to bring people to focus within their own hearts for God, their attention is draw to priests and bishops and popes who, somehow, someway, have a special messenger service to God, and therefore, must lead the ignorant people to God through their magical power.

But then, all the clerics would be out

of a job if people began to realize that they are just as much priests as anyone else. The role of the priest should not be to take the people to God via their special powers, but rather to help people use their own resources to find God. This may be a subtle distinction at times, but paramount, nonetheless, for true spiritual growth. This is the way a true spiritual leader works. If people came to him and say put us in touch with God, he says "put yourself in touch. I'll give you a few hints and tips, but you and you alone can find God. No one can find him for you and deposit him in your heart."

And so Bishop, I could write on and on and on about my dissatisfaction with the Church on both a theological and practical level, but I'm sure that you're as weary from reading this as my hand is from writing it. So I will leave you with these few thoughts in hope that you won't dismiss my decision as just another fatality of the secular city without considering the effect the position of the Church today has had on my decision. The Church today is simply not the Church Christ spoke of or envisioned.

Two years ago I was willing to devote my entire life to serving others through the ordained priesthood, but now I see I would be of no real service at all if the people have not reached a personal freedom and deepened spirituality. I honestly don't think the Church allows this. In fact, I believe it discourages people from truly confronting themselves. Most catholics are still waiting around for their orders. And as long as the priest-layman relationship remains as it is, they will continue to wait, and they will not be disappointed. I won't assume responsibility for others, thinking that I'm being of service to them.

And finally, because I believe as mahaatma Ghandhi did that "a man who says that religion has nothing to do with politics does not know what religion is," I've taken a drastic step to eradicate myself from the immoral policies of our government in Vietnam and other areas and to show my opposition to the unconstitutional and un-democratic Selective Service System. I have returned my draft cards to my local board explaining that I will not complete my two years of alternative service because no man should be forced into service for his country either as a soldier or as a conscientous objector. Furthermore, the Selective Service System and the army are not two separate institutions. The Army is designed primarily to achieve military victory through the destruction of other human beings. The Selective Service System merely feeds the army, providing it with tools of destruction — soldiers. I cannot be part of this destructive unit. And so, I await prosecution and prison, which seem likely at this point, knowing that if because of my action even one man vows never to be violent again toward a fellow human being, it will have been worth it.

Shalom,
Om Shanti,
Michael Gillotti

3. Letter to Bishop Dingman, 1980

March 1, 1980

Michael A. Gillotti
1145 B Dutch Lane
Penngrove, CA 95451

Bishop Maurice Dingman
Diocese of Des Moines
2010 Grand
Des Moines, Iowa 50306

Dear Bishop Dingman and all the clergy of the Des Moines Diocese,

I have recently completed repayment of my seminarian loan accrued while attending Loras College from 1966 to 1970. I would like to use this as an opportunity to not only complete my financial obligation but also to complete my relationship with you, as bishop, and with the Diocese of Des Moines in general.

Nearly ten years ago, when I left the formal seminary, I wrote you a very impassioned and at times caustic letter condemning you and the Catholic Church and offering an explanation of why I left the seminary. I was very angry, and in some ways it is understandable that I did not receive a response from you. This time I am hoping to engage you in a dialogue and invite you to respond.

First of all I want to acknowledge the fact that my years in the seminary were very valuable years. I consider it an opportunity to have been engaged in the process of learning how to serve others as Christ did and in removing the barriers I had to truly serving others and not just myself. This has been an invaluable experience which I carry into my everyday life even now.

There are two specific issues I would like to discuss with you which concern me very deeply: 1.) The Catholic Church's role in assisting men and women in their spiritual growth and in their finding freedom of spirit, love, happiness and fulfillment. Or, in other words, how the Catholic Church contributes or not to people's lives being truly satisfying and having vitality. 2.) The role of the Catholic Church in relation to war, the military, the draft, nuclear weapons etc.

In regard to no.1, the ultimate question seems to be what are the results? Are people experiencing a greater degree of wellbeing, love and happiness as a result of their participation with the church? Are people's lives enriched? Is there aliveness, vitality, peace and freedom of spirit? Certainly there are some Catholics for which these things are present. But as I look around I see that most people's lives don't work very well. They are unhappy, have a very low self-esteem, there is little true love in their lives and freedom of spirit and peace are infrequent visitors. This is not to blame the Church for people's lives not working or for their unhappiness, but rather to note that the church has not been effective in responding to their condition. How long will we delude ourselves that the Church is having the impact on people's lives that we'd like it to.

It is my experience that people are never really free unless they are free to fully experience life and allow life itself to be their teacher. Another way of saying this is that in order to truly learn the lessons of life and of successful living, we must be free to make mistakes and to learn from them as well. We must arrive at the answers ourselves. And we must trust in our experiences, trust in life itself to teach us what it is we are to know. Actually, there are really no mistakes, since everything we experience contributes to our learning. This, I think, in the most literal sense is faith, and not as we have been taught, belief in something to be true because someone says it's so.

It is in this area of "freedom" and "faith" that I think the Church has failed profoundly. Instead of freedom of spirit and faith, we are taught to be slaves and to mistrust our own experience. We are taught to be "careful" to be "cautious" rather than to go out into life and let life teach us what it will. The result is an incredible stifling of the human spirit, of spontaneity and affection. Even now at many masses and liturgies this death of the spirit is apparent, as well as in people's everyday lives. We must always be on guard so as not to sin or do wrong, and this cautiousness creates tension or tightness which strangles the human spirit.

So the Church, it seems to me becomes a major obstacle rather than an aid to attaining freedom, faith, love and peace. This is one reason I left the seminary. I did not want, as a priest, to be an obstacle to other's growth.

Further, it is my experience that spiritual growth, freedom, peace and love are not attained until a person takes responsibility for his or her own life and spirituality. Most, it seems, defer this responsibility to the priest, bishop, pope etc. Most say to the priest, "you tell me the answers. You show me the way. You save me." They do not look within themselves but search outside themselves for someone to give it to them. In this respect priests and the Church are also obstacles to people's growth.

2.) The second issue is one of the Church's relationship to war, the military, the draft and nuclear weapons. I heard Father Dan Berrigan talk last night and he reminded me of one of my deepest disappointments during the Vietnam War, which also contributed greatly to my leaving the seminary. That is the failure of the Catholic Church to speak out strongly and passionately to condemn the United States for our immoral and murderous involvement in Vietnam. If there is one institution in the world which should be unequivocally and uncompromisingly opposed to war in any form it is the Church. If the Church doesn't take such a stand who will?

I ask you, will you again be silent as we approach another bloody confrontation? Will you say "We must defend our country" even if this means destroying other human beings, perhaps all human beings. Father Berrigan said there is one thing he is always clear about. This is the commandment, "Thou shall not kill." Thou shall not destroy life. Also, we are human beings first and American citizens second.

I encourage you and support you this time to take a more active role in resisting the growing military spirit in this country. I encourage you to actively and passionately discourage young men and women from registering for the draft. I encourage you to "ex-communicate" any Catholics who actually support war or the draft in any form. I encourage you to use your position as bishop to push for a reduction of the military budget and the use of that money for constructive purposes.

I plead with you to recognize the urgency of reducing and eliminating nuclear weapons (we now have over 30,000 nuclear weapons stockpiled capable of unthinkable human destruction). Now more than ever there is no winnable war. We all lose, and perhaps we all die this time. Please, please bring Christ's message of love and of respect for life into the world in such a way that all that hear it will see that it is impossible to be a Christian and at the same time be a soldier in attitude or in action.

Sincerely,
Michael Gillotti

4. Letter from Bishop Dingman in response to my letter of 1980.

DIOCESE OF DES MOINES / P.O. BOX 1816 · 2910 GRAND AVENUE · DES MOINES, IOWA 50306

June 23, 1980

THE CHANCERY

Mr. Michael A. Gillotti
1145 B Dutch Lane
Penngrove, California 94951

Dear Michael:

Time has gotten away from me. I received your letter of March 1st and fully intended to respond much sooner than this. Please excuse my delay.

The issues you raise in your letter are of personal concern to me. I think that my record in the Diocese of Des Moines will speak for itself in attesting to my concern with the spiritual growth of all the men and women of this diocese and my concern for the Church in relationship to war and the arms race. I know that I could do more. I search each day for ways in which to strengthen my commitment to both of these areas.

I find it difficult to respond to your letter in writing. What would be a great privilege for me would be to have the opportunity to visit with you in person. I am not sure how frequently you return to the Des Moines area, but I wish to invite you at this time to come and visit with me about your concerns the next time you are in Des Moines. This would please me greatly. I do believe that we think along similar lines and could benefit greatly from an opportunity to dialogue face to face.

May I add a personal note of thanks for having repaid to the Diocese the money which was loaned to you as a seminarian. Your willingness to take care of this matter will help us to be able to extend the help of the Diocese to those who are preparing for Priesthood. I appreciate that this may have been an extra sacrifice for you. Be assured of my gratitude.

With hopes that we can have a visit in the not too distant future, I am

Sincerely yours in Christ,

† Maurice Dingman

Most Rev. Maurice J. Dingman
Bishop of Des Moines

5. Letter from Father Danial Berrigan in response to
my Letter to Bishop Dingman, 1980.
(I had sent Fr. Berrigan a copy of Bishop Dingman's letter)

Dear Michael —

Thanks for that good letter to the bishop. He's one of the better ones. I stayed at his home in des Moines + liked him greatly.

I hope we're not merely telling others what to do, but doing something ourselves?

Love

Dan Berrigan

6. Newspaper article in the Des Moines Register Aug. 1985 where Bishop Dingman condemns the Contra war.

Thurs., Aug. 15, 1985 ■ THE DES MOINES REGISTER / 3A

Dingman, other clerics assail U.S. contra aid

Maurice Dingman of the Des Moines Roman Catholic Diocese, calling on President Reagan to "please let the people of Nicaragua alone," Wednesday joined six other religious leaders in a slashing attack on the Reagan administration's support of rebel forces in Nicaragua.

The clergy blamed the U.S. government for acts of torture, rape, kidnap and murder against civilians in the Central American country, and said the Reagan administration is lying about its role there.

The war in Nicaragua is "a national sin and a disgrace," said the Rev. Jim Wallis of the Sojourners Community.

Dingman decried American support for Nicaraguan rebels, and urged the United States to consult the World Court, the United Nations or some other outside mediator.

Fact-finding Visits

The clergy were here to support Witness for Peace, an ecumenical religious organization that crusades against American policies in Nicaragua and sends U.S. citizens there on fact-finding visits. The group gained worldwide attention last week when 29 Americans on such a trip said they were kidnapped and held for a day before being released.

Although there were conflicting reports about the identity of the kidnappers, a Witness for Peace staff member said the evidence points to a group called the Revolutionary Democratic Alliance, known by the acronym

Maurice Dingman
A duty to speak out

to overthrow the leftist government of Nicaragua.

Ed Griffin-Nolan, who was among the 29 detained Americans, said the captors "identified themselves from the beginning as members of ARDE." Leaders of that rebel group have denied the charge.

About 1,300 Americans have toured Nicaragua under Witness for Peace sponsorship, and group adviser Dick Taylor said the trips will continue into war zones — despite warnings from the State Department. "We know that there are risks in a war zone," he said. "But we believe that those who work for peace must be willing to take the same risks as those who fight in war."

In a statement, Taylor blamed the U.S. government for a barrage of of atrocities by terrorists who "mutilate innocent people, kill children, burn

Continued next page

Dingman, other clerics assail U.S. on Contra aid

Continued from previous page

down health clinics and schools, torture people in front of their families and commit horrors almost too atrocious to describe.

"Terrorism and Brutality"

"As Christians, as Jews, as American citizens, we cannot sit by while our tax money is used to support such terrorism and brutality."

Dingman said one of his saddest days was July 26, when he learned that Congress had agreed to spend $27 million on non-military aid to Nicaragua that will be used to assist the rebel forces. "Please let those people of Nicaragua alone," implored Dingman. "Let them solve their problems as they see best. . . ."

In questioning, the clergy acknowledged that they could claim no religious consensus on American policy in Nicaragua. But Dingman said he and his colleagues had to say their piece nevertheless.

"I spent four years in Rome in 1936 to 1940, and I've always believed that if the bishops of Germany and Italy had spoken out, many of the war atrocities never would have come about," he said.

"I think the religious community has to speak out, to be the conscience to the nation."

Besides Dingman and Wallis, religious leaders who appeared at the news conference were Roman Catholic Bishops Walter Sullivan of Richmond, Va., and Thomas Gumbleton of Detroit, Mich.; the Rev. Avery Post, president of the United Church of Christ; Sister Joan Chittister, president of the conference of American Benedictine Prioresses; and Rabbi Balfour Brickner of the Stephen Wise Free Synagogue in New York City.

7. Letter to Bishop Dingman, 1985, congratulating him on his stand against the Contra War.

Sept. 5, 1985

Bishop Maurice Dingman
C/O Diocese Of Des Moines

Michael Gillotti
6979 Baker Ln.
Sebastopol, CA 95472

Dear Bishop Dingman,

Last week my mother sent me an article from the Des Moines paper in which you took a public stand against our governments policy in Nicaragua, and in particular our support of the murderous and brutal Contras. I'm writing at this time to loudly and enthusiastically applaud and acknowledge you for taking this position, a stand that puts you in direct opposition to Reagan and, in some ways, apparently, the Pope.

You may remember that several years ago, when I decided to discontinue my preparation for the priesthood, I wrote a very scathing letter to you denouncing the church and you for not taking stronger stands on such issues, particularly the Vietnam War, nuclear weapons and war in general. I can't tell you how thrilled I am to see the statements that you and other leaders have been making. You have my wholehearted support.

I too share your deep sadness and disgust for U.S. policy which desecrates innocent human beings through it surrogate mercenary soldiers. It was out of compassion and anger that I signed the Pledge of Resistance this Spring, pledging to commit civil disobedience if Reagan escalates the war in Nicaragua; and it was this same compassion that lead me to participate in a non-violent demonstration in May in which myself and 80 others were arrested for blockading the Marine Recruitment center in Santa Rosa. I recently completed serving 2 days in the county jail, a minor inconvenience that I gladly accepted in hope that it might make some small difference. I simply felt, as you did, that I had to take a stand.

Though I believe strongly that each individual must take responsibility for him or herself and for the larger community, and that this is the basis for true community and lasting change, I also recognize that those in leadership roles, such as yourself, do have a tremendous impact on the larger community by awakening their consciences. At the very least, it's a real morale booster to those of us "down in the trenches", so to speak. Thank You Again!

Finally, I'm enclosing a copy of song, Take Me To Your Border, from my second album, Heartlove, which I recently completely, but as yet is unreleased. Please feel free to use it in any way you think might useful. (I also put on a copy of a second song, Old Woman, that I thought you might enjoy).

I hope this finds you in good health.

In Peace,

Michael Gillotti

8. A few of Swami Satchidananda's Questions and Answers from early Yoga Retreats.

QUESTION: How can I truly know without any doubt that God is with me every moment? So often it seems that I am alone and on my own.

ANSWER: God is with you every second. If not, you wouldn't even be living. This is the proof: in order to live, you have to breathe. Are you breathing consciously every minute? Who is making you breathe? The One who wants you to live. And that's what you call God. Yes. Breathing itself is not in your hands. If you forget to breathe, God will make you breathe. Even if you don't want to breathe, God will force you to breathe. Can you exhale and stop breathing? No. The air is forced back into the body. Who does that? Somebody is interested in your living. God is in you, working through your body and mind every minute. There's no doubt about it. Believe in that, and allow God's hand to work through you. Your life will be better, easier and more happy. You are never alone. God is nearer to you than your own heart.

QUESTION: How should we pray? There seems to be a contradiction between totally trusting in God's Will and praying for someone or something.

ANSWER: It is the same thing. There is no contradiction at all. But you should understand the purpose of your prayer. You don't go and ask God, "Give me that." If you feel you must ask for something, then say, "Please give me understanding. Give me the constant remembrance that You are handling everything, that You will give me everything I deserve, and You will never give anything to me if I don't deserve it." If God is going to do something only after you request it, what kind of God is that? "Oh, because ten people are praying for you, because I got ten thousand signatures, I am giving you this." No. But when ten thousand people feel sorry for a person and pray, all that wishful thinking goes to help him or her.

Good thoughts and feelings always reach the ones who are really starving for them. Those who really deserve that good thinking will receive it. We simply spread the seeds. When people know that so many others are praying for them, that gives them strength. There is a benefit right away, "Oh, so many people are praying for me. I should really get well. All their good thinking is on my side." Prayerful thoughts always bring benefit to people.

QUESTION: How do you keep from worrying about the future? Sometimes I can't sleep I have so much worry about what might happen.

ANSWER: What you sow you reap. Don't worry about the future and don't worry about the past. A great thinker said the past and the future are not even visible. But what is visible? The golden present. Think of the golden present, sow what is necessary, what is right. Sow good thoughts, sow good deeds, and I am sure you will reap good fruits. There is no question about it. What you do comes back to you. What you sow you reap. So do the right thing in the present, and don't worry about the future. The people who worry about the future miss the present as well. You have something right now. You have it in the hand, something nice to eat: don't think, "What will happen if I am hungry tomorrow?" By the time you find that out someone will have come and snatched it from you. Always remember the golden present.

Never miss it. A happier life is not given to you by someone else. Not even God can give you a happier life. Remember that. Happiness is in you. If you take care not to lose it, it is always there.

61070788R00105

Made in the USA
Charleston, SC
15 September 2016